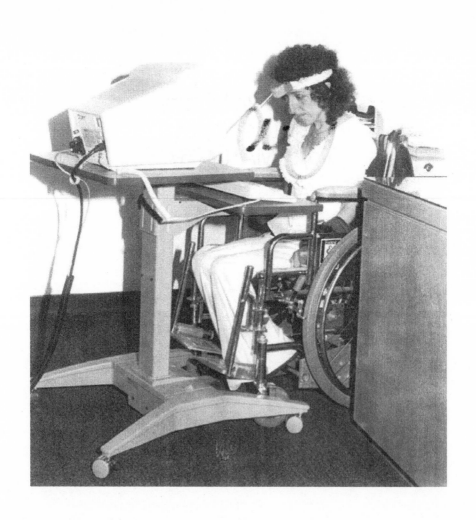

Beyond The Wheelchair

Welcome To My World

By

Gail Sanfilippo

Order this book online at www.trafford.com
or email orders@trafford.com

Most Trafford titles are also available at major online book retailers.

Printed in the United States of America.

ISBN: 978-1-4269-4348-5 (sc)
ISBN: 978-1-4269-4349-2 (e)
ISBN: 978-1-4269-4350-8 (hc)

Library of Congress Control Number: 2010913585

*Our mission is to efficiently provide the world's finest, most comprehensive book publishing
service, enabling every author to experience success. To find out how to publish your book,
your way, and have it available worldwide, visit us online at www.trafford.com*

Trafford rev. 11/22/2010

 www.trafford.com

North America & international
toll-free: 1 888 232 4444 (USA & Canada)
phone: 250 383 6864 • fax: 812 355 4082

"BEYOND THE WHEELCHAIR"

BY: GAIL SANFILIPPO

INTRODUCTION

My story begins in 1953, May 6 to be exact, and I'll share it in two parts. The first part is from birth to my college graduation at age 30 and the second part covers my life from the time when I moved out of my parents' home at age 32 and started living independently. I will show how growing up in a loving and supportive family environment based on sacrifice has given me roots in which I grew up in fertile soil to be the successful woman I am today. Despite my handicap, I have an amazing story to tell. Even Oprah has nothing on me! The beginning may have been rough, but it's been an astonishing path I traveled down.

Readers will find I've had a host of hurdles to overcome, but with the love and support of my family I have become a woman who is living independently, a college graduate, and author of a book that will help change your outlook on life. Lessons and inner strength from my youth played a strong role when I became independent. Coupled with natural instincts, these lessons helped me develop wisdom to go along with the feelings in my heart. My reason and my emotions took me on roads only I traveled.

When I moved out and started living on my own I started to use the lessons I learned in my youth - to rely on my inner strength and my natural instincts, to grow in wisdom using what I possess in my head and my heart, my reason and my emotions. I will also describe to the best of what my memory permits an accurate description of my life and what it means to have no alternative but to have to depend on other people for everything. Acts taken for granted by others such as placing my feet on the floor to get up out of bed in the morning, washing my face, brushing my teeth and going to the bathroom are some things I will never be able to do for myself. I even need to rely on others to eat. Unfor-tunately, I have come to the harsh reality that people, even my family and relatives, basically do not understand what I go through during a single day.

I was born three weeks early on May 6, 1953, a seven pounds, thirteen ounce little girl at Melrose-Wakefield Hospital, Massachusetts. The doctor who delivered me was not my mother's first choice. We had our own family physician who delivered both my brother and my sister. I, being the first born, suffered the penalty of my mother's choice to listen to the guidance of one of her older sisters. I later learned that my Mom was petrified about having a baby and took her older sister's recommendations and used a different doctor instead of her own to deliver me. I was in the breach position in my mother's womb so the doctor who delivered me used forceps to pull me out in order to speed up my delivery. Little did my parents know what these actions of Dr. Johnson's would develop into for the next fifty-five years of their daughter's life. For whatever reason, neither Dr. Johnson nor his staff was forthcoming about the damage he did. They did not come forward and truthfully tell my parents what happened, instead telling them that their first born baby girl had little to no chance of survival. I found out fifty-three years later that I was deprived of oxygen for twelve minutes, triple the time needed to cause brain damage! And I was three weeks early. I should have been severely retarded or dead. I learned decades later I was the last newborn this doctor ever delivered by his choice. God must have compensated for my disability when He gave me a spirit as lofty as cirrus clouds and as tough as a lightning strike (much to the chagrin of not only my mother but many people who have met me in this life) .

This was not the only painful experience this doctor left stamped on my mother's psyche. In the 1950's the subject of sexual harassment was not a topic the judicial system knew how to deal with. Women who were subjected to this kind of harassment by so called professionals were never taken seriously, and were actually made to feel like the guilty party. So it was for my mother during her monthly scheduled examinations with the doctor when she was touched in inappropriate ways.

In response to the doctor's dismal analysis I was baptized as Mary Sanfilippo while still in the incubator in the Natal Intensive Care Unit of the hospital, daughter of Ignazio Lawrence and Edna May Sanfilippo. They named me Mary initially because Catholic tradition dictated that baby girls who were going to depart this life be named after the Virgin Mary to go without human intervention up to heaven. In the days to follow, my parents started to make the funeral arrangements while I remained in the nursery hooked up to various life support machines keeping me alive. I have been told that by all outward appearances I seemed healthy, even though I looked like a puppet on a string in the Natal Intensive Care Unit. I have seen pictures to support this description. I cannot possibly imagine my parents having any idea how strong willed I was as I laid there during my infancy. It didn't take but a few weeks before I was able to be released from the hospital looking like a healthy baby girl. Little did I know the fight of my life was only just beginning! I was baptized again in St. Anthony's, a Catholic church in Everett, Massachusetts where my family lived. This time, however, I was baptized as Gail Sanfilippo. My parents decided to raise me a Catholic, as they did for my brother and sister, instead of my mother's Baptist religion.

For the first three to five years of my life I was in and out of hospital clinics being studied and examined by doctors and interns because I had not yet been diagnosed with Cerebral Palsy and my parents needed to have an answer to why their baby daughter was not starting to sit up or maneuver her tiny hands to hold a bottle or spoon to eat. They wondered why I was not swarming and trying to stand as other babies my age were doing. I did not have the fine motor skills that most babies come into this world with and was not even able to suck on a bottle. The front doors and main entrances of the numerous medical facilities I was carried thru in the arms of my mother became more familiar than my own front door. Even at that toddler stage I was very aware of what was going on around me and will never forget the cold steel examination tables and my tiny body teetering on the edge as my arms and legs were so spastic that I had no control over where they moved. Young men and women in long white attire with strange looking instruments hanging around their necks would hit my knees with a hammer as they stood around the table I was wobbling on. They all had such curious looks on their faces as they whispered amongst themselves that they had me believing I looked like some monster people would pay to see in a circus; a freak of nature. This memory is as clear today as when it happened, over fifty years ago.

This was a really odd feeling to me because at home I was looked upon as normal while all my aunts and uncles would fawn and coo over me as they all held me. From the pictures I have since seen of myself as a baby, I really was cute as my mother held me on her lap at the holiday dinner tables. When I was about three and a half years old I was diagnosed with Cerebral Palsy.

Cerebral Palsy (CP) is a group of motor problems and physical disorders related to a brain injury. CP causes uncontrolled reflex movements and muscle tightness, called spasticity that may affect a part, a side, or the entire body with varying degrees of severity. Many other conditions such as mental retardation, seizures, or vision and hearing problems, are often associated with CP.

There are several causes of Cerebral Palsy. The main cause is the deprivation of blood, oxygen, or other nutrients before or during birth. Second, complications related to being born premature. Third, a head injury. Fourth, developing a serious infection or high fever, such as meningitis.

There are three types of Cerebral Palsy: spastic, athetoid and ataxic. Spastic is the most common. A child with spastic Cerebral Palsy cannot relax his/her muscles or the muscles may be stiff.

Athetoid Cerebral Palsy affects the child's ability to control the muscles of the body, thus muscles may flutter and move suddenly.

Ataxic Cerebral Palsy causes problems with balance and coordination.*

I was diagnosed with both spastic and athetoid cerebral palsy.

My parents had never heard of this disability and neither had approximately ninety-five percent of the population back then. My parents knew one thing for sure. They would raise their first-born daughter in a loving home, surrounded by love and nurturing no matter what they had to sacrifice along the way. And so my life had the chance to evolve just like my brother and sister's did. Here was the first step in my long journey.

PART ONE

THE EARLY YEARS

CHAPTER ONE

MY FAMILY TREE

My Grandfather Francesco Sanfilippo, whom I called Papa, came from Sicily as a young man. Previous to this, in his youth, after the age of eighteen he was enlisted in the Italian Navy which in turn drafted him into the Army. His family came sporadically to America in the twentieth century, between the years of 1910 and 1925. As a young man here in America he took work on fishing boats out of both Boston and Gloucester and came home from fishing trips loaded down with flounder, cod and a fish called skate which looks similar to a stingray with wings and a long pointed tail. The meat inside the wings tasted like scallops. Our cellar was set up with a freezer in which Papa stored the fish until he cleaned and scaled what Nana wanted to cook for dinner. He became the Captain of the dragger "Little Nancy." In October of 1953 (the year I was born), his boat burned and sank offshore. When the crew was rescued, my Uncle Mac and my grandfather were using oars to steer the dory but it took on water so fast that it could not be turned. In an attempt to follow in his father's footsteps, my father did try his hand at fishing but he was not able to overcome his propensity for seasickness on the choppy New England waters.

My patriarchal grandmother, Agnes Ciula, was born in America in 1908. As I understand from my Auntie Lilly, who is my father's sister, when my Papa came to America there was an old custom to visit people they know. I presumed he came here to America to get married and some people he knew did have a daughter. Marriages back then were prearranged. So when my Papa visited the girl he discovered that she was a very heavy woman and not at all attractive to him. Her family gave him two beautiful gifts, a gold coin, worth thousands today , and a gold watch. In between these visits, my Papa stopped over to visit my Nana's parents and as he was entering the house, he saw this other girl hanging cloths. When he went into the house, he asked who she was and so I guess it was love at first sight, because my Papa told the father of the other girl he loved someone else and could not marry her .

My father was born in November 28, 1927 at home in Boston's North End and brought up in Everett. He came from a large family of Italian descent and graduated from Everett Vocational High School in 1945.

My mother, who was born two years later in Everett, graduated from Everett High and worked in the payroll department of F.W. Dodge. My mother was very smart when it came to anything having to do with math and accounting. After graduation she went to work for Sears and Roebuck. She continued to work after she married my father and only stopped working a couple of weeks or so before I was born.

My parents first met in December of 1948 at a friend's Christmas party, although they had grown up in the same city and lived there all of their lives.

From the start my father showed interest in my mother but he joined the Army and went over to Korea as a military policeman (MP) for about a year and a half, leaving his job at General Electric. Their courtship never actually started until 1949. They dated once a week for awhile, but this relationship did not work out well in the beginning. Jealousy can do many things, so my father gave up being out with his buddies. Dates were always after my Dad got off from his three to eleven o'clock shift at General Electric which was in Lynn, Massachusetts. Sometimes they just met in my Grandparent Campbell's living room on Reed Street, Everett, Massachusetts and just talked until it got light out. My mother tells a funny story about this happening when my Nana Campbell, being so lenient due to her overly disciplined childhood, used to creep downstairs whispering to my Mother "Your father's coming down very shortly." I guess then all three made a mad disappearing act, scurrying to their proper places before my Grandfather came downstairs for breakfast.

My Mom told me of this other hilarious incident which occurred while she was dating my Dad . It seems that whenever the two of them went out in the car, my Dad pulled over a lot telling my Mom the tire had to be checked. It was not until their wedding night when my Dad passed wind saying "I've been suffering, Edna, for the past three years!"

My parents, being from two different religious and ethnic backgrounds, did not help their courtship either. My Dad was Catholic and of Italian descent and with my Mother being of Protestant and French, English and Scotch heritage surely did not help. My grandfather on my mother's side did not take too well to his daughter marrying a Catholic. As my Mother tells me, my Father was willing to convert to the Protestant faith.

My Mother told me years later about the first time my Dad brought my Mom's parents over to meet his parents. My Grandfather Campbell nearly fainted when my father met him because, like the rest of his family, my dad had a boisterous, happy go lucky nature and was such a cheerful man. It was very funny to me, because I could picture my Grandfather Campbell, as reserved and soft-spoken as he was, being appalled at the loud and happy man that would inevitably become a part of his family. The two were exact opposites.

Despite the disapproval of Grandpa, my parents were married on a rainy day on May 25, 1952. My Father footed the bill for the wedding, and he bought my mother her wedding gown.

My Father worked thirty-eight years for General Electric at the Lynn and Everett, Massachusetts plants. He started out as a custodian sweeping floors before he married my mother and during their marriage worked his way up to welding parts for aircraft carriers. Throughout the duration of his service to General Electric he was laid off a lot (as all the blue collar workers were from time to time). During these times he found other jobs driving tar trucks and serving on the Everett police force. When General Electric called him back, these jobs would overlap at times. The last job he worked at before his retirement in 1987 was as a welder for aircraft engines. He loved the work and I heard that co-workers used to ask him to check for cracks on their engines prior to their departure to the assembly line.

While they were waiting for the apartment downstairs from my Dad's parents' house to be renovated and remodeled, my parents stayed at both of my grandparents' houses in Everett or down on Cape Cod at a rented cottage which my maternal Grandparents had for the summer. From my math it was in that time frame that I was conceived, either in Everett or down at Cape Cod at one of the cottages!

When my mother was pregnant with me, they moved into the renovated apartment on the first floor of the half of a house which Papa Sanfilippo owned. My grandparents had the whole apartment renovated because they wanted to be close to their son and daughter-in-law. The other half was owned by other family relatives. My aunts, uncles and cousins on my father's side lived in the same dwelling upstairs with only two or three bedrooms. Looking back now, I wonder how my Grandparents had any privacy with six children around. But this is how a lot of families grew up seventy or so years ago. In addition to my Papa and Nana's duplex, there two others that were occupied with even more of my Dad's relatives as first, second and even third generations of cousins, so I grew up in a very tight family environment. Throughout the years when my father's sisters Auntie Lillian and Auntie Josie were married, they, too, resided on Vine Street for a period of years, so I really grew up with many family values.

The way we thought of her, my Nana Sanfilippo was a typical old fashioned Italian grandmother with always plenty of food for all of us. She always cooked enough to feed a small army! She was an amazingly warm, heavy-set woman, always cooking up mouth-watering old fashioned meals at our home on Vine Street, where she lived upstairs. She had always taken a lot of pride in her family as well as helping out others who needed a helping hand . She took such great pride in her matriarchal position in the family and fulfilling her purpose in life. She usually had on a house dress and printed apron as she stood at her stove frying up the meatballs and pork chops (and on "special" occasions pigs feet for flavor, which repelled me at the time!) . She made the dinner in her cast iron skillet, while the sauce she had put together to use with her tomato sauce (which we called "gravy") was like some kind of magic potion to which only she knew the ingredients, simmered for hours on the other burner .

Each Sunday morning my Nana Sanfilippo would call down from the head landing of the upstairs and shout downstairs "Iggie, come up to get Gail's fried meatballs, gravy and Italian roll." My Dad, being his own standup comedian always said "What about me? I'm you're son!" My Nana continued to say quite sincerely "Gail is more important!" Sundays at one o'clock was like open house at Nana Sanfilippo's with aunts, uncles, cousins and guests, drawn to the smell of food cooking and a mixture of Italian or pop music flowing out from my grandparents' huge hi-fi ,which was in the hallway next to the kitchen , and sports blaring from the front living room where all the men gathered in between the main meal and dessert. No one starved or had worms. The garlic killed everything!

And, of course, there was always wine on the table. It still brings to mind someone mixing for me a quarter of this appalling port red wine with orange soda to cut the taste of it at and coffee with biscotti (Italian cookies made from flour, sugar, eggs, almonds and vanilla) at every Sunday dinner.

Most every other Thursday it was chicken soup day when all my cousins, aunts and uncles gathered at her kitchen table to eat the "best" soup ever. As usual, my grand-mother put together her homemade chicken soup which was accompanied by the best fried chicken I have ever had topped with fried onions. My grandmother was always very surprised by the amount of food I put away when she cooked, but she knew how much I enjoyed her fried chicken and onions. It was one of my most favorite meals that my Nana cooked. I used to get three thirds of the fried onions automatically right from the sizzling, frying pan.

Two of my favorite dishes were my Nana's garlic macaroni she made on occasion from spaghetti with freshly diced cloves of garlic, virgin olive oil an recently grated cheese.

The second was her fish soup made from fish heads, olive oil, cloves of garlic and tons of freshly grated cheese. When I ever heard in later years that she used fish heads, I said "No!" Just the idea of eating the liquid from fishes' brains made me sick to my stomach, but there are some things one needs to put back in one's mind. Just think about China and Japan's food and delicacies! They actually sell and eat dog. I know I would starve to death, but these are the customs. All I can say is that nobody could ever duplicate Nana's recipes. She held secrets that would always be secrets and these two she carried to her grave.

Nana was a simple woman and her whole existence was her family. My memories of her are varied like the patterns of her aprons. I will never forget when she had taken care of me while my Mother went to the hospital to give birth to my sister, Nancy. It is one I will cherish forever. I was always being fed with stories to make me eat. One I remember more than others was that she told me she would bring me to the circus if I ate. Apparently the circus overlooked the children of Everett, because I waited for years and was beginning to grow heavier and heavier! This one statement was all she ever said and she continued on for years with each of her grandchildren until we were old enough to know that she had no intention of bringing me or any other of her grandkids to the circus. To be sure, my Nana's method worked, because my Mother told me that when she saw me after she came home from the hospital she did not recognize me since I had gained so much weight. Yes, food was love to my Nana Sanfilippo.

Nana was a very religious woman. Often while my grandmother was standing at the stove, I could hear her whispering the rosary under her breath to herself over and over again. This never made sense to me, because I always was told that God was everywhere and sees everything, so why did he need to hear prayer upon prayer? When I was around eight or so, she started taking me to The Fisherman's Feast in the North End of Boston.

Since 1911, "The Fisherman's Feast" has been an event every year based on the devotion of the fishermen from Sciacca to the Soccorso (Our Lady of Help) which lasts for four days with the blessing of the fishing waters and food. The favorite dishes are Italian sausages, calamari, pizza and pasta. The finale of the feast is on Sunday night with "Flight of the Angel."*

Nana's nurturing skills and religious beliefs could be seen as she pushed me down North Street and Fleet Street in these sticky "dog days" of August. Not only was I sweating my ass off, but I felt so uncomfortable in my own skin at this age being in a wheelchair. Men, women, young and old, and children, were tossing dollar bills of every denomination down off their apartments minute to give praise to this statue in the hopes that a prayer would be answered or a miracle would touch their lives. I found out later the statue was the image of the Madonna DiAnzano, also known as Our Lady of Help, who was discovered four hundred years ago in a tiny village now called Anzano, Sicily.

The legend is that, when a farmer's cow wandered away, and as he searched for him, the farmer saw a beam of light upon some shrubs which was in the form of the Madonna. The statue was erected in a nearby town of Trevico, in the honor of this discovery. As the sculpture was lifted onto a wagon with a single bull pulling it, the wagon could not be moved, so the people decided they needed additional bulls to move it. At last, a total of nine bulls brought the figure to the border of Trevico, and no further. A chapel was built at the spot where the statue of Madonna still stands today.

When I was growing up I could see that my Nana Sanfilippo had very few pleasures in her life. One of them was having the women in the neighborhood coming over to play cards once a week. Living downstairs, I could hear the clicking of shoes above me when someone won and, of course, my grandmother's footsteps continuously pacing back and forth on the tiled kitchen floor getting food and beverages for her guests.

As her family grew and went our own ways my Nana took up Bingo. I believe these digressions, which took place two nights weekly at both a local Catholic Church hall and Jewish synagogue, kept her going. Oh, how she loved Bingo! I well remember during the weeks, months and years she persistently said "I only had one number to go before winning a thousand or so!"

Despite my belief that my maternal grandparents came from totally different back-grounds, I am finding out in writing this book that they were a lot alike. My Grandfather Thomas Campbell and Grandmother Catherine Frigout had grown up in the same neighborhood near Kent, England. As for my Grandpa Campbell, his mother died in childbirth leaving him to be raised by his Aunt Jessie who was a very strict woman, so I am told. My grandfather's father married three times, with his first wife dying, the second he divorced, and the third residing with him in Malden, Massachusetts until her death.

My Nana Campbell grew up in a very affluent neighborhood over in England. She told me that she often played with the children at Buckingham Palace. Her mother was a very controlling woman who never approved of the young men she dated. She also had drinking problems, which drove my Grandmother further away.

World War One was being fought around the time that my grandfather met my grandmother. He did not believe in the war, but he served as a cook in the British military. From the stories my grandmother told me, they were deeply in love but because of her mother's iron fist they made secret plans to meet up with each other in America. They both made a vow to meet in five years to get married in America.

In five years my Grandmother left in the middle of the night to make her great escape from her mother's overwhelming protectiveness to get the ship to America to meet my Grampa Campball and never look back again. As I was told, my Great Grandfather Campbell was already in America employed as a wallpaper designer, which was a very good job in those days. He owned a couple of houses down on Cape Cod and gave an automobile to his son and daughter-in-law who were the first people in the neighborhood with a car.

After they married, my maternal grandparents had six children in all: five girls and one boy, but the first baby, Irene, died in my Grandmother's arms. I will never know that type of feeling of loss, but only can imagine. My Nana always told me that if my aunt had lived, she would have had been like me, but in reality she never really knew the true cause of my aunt's sudden death. Cerebral Palsy was an unknown term, even less so eighty-three years ago than it was five decades ago when I was born.

My Aunt Joan was the second daughter born after Irene. She got married in 1945 to my Uncle Charlie Kelley and they were not able to have a child for fourteen years, so we were treated like royalty, treated like their own children, throughout this approximate decade and a half . Every Friday evening my aunt and uncle came to visit us with all kinds of surprises which always came along with candy and a card game of Pokeno or Uno. Pokeno consisted of twelve large game boards with pictures of 25 cards. The object of the game was to win chips if one got the four corners, the four of a kind or a straight. Each of us had our favorite Pokeno card or cards. Mine was with the four sevens on it. Sometimes we played until midnight after my Dad went to work routinely questioning my Mom upon the location of his keys and hat. "Where are my car keys and hat, Edna?" This was my Dad's nightly ritual around twenty minutes to eleven five nights a week, week in and week out as if my Mom had a magnet on her. Then a big disclosure in the summer of 1959 , when in the middle of a family gathering at my Uncle Gordon's home in West Yarmouth while kids were screaming and running around ,when my Aunt Joanie blurted out "There might be another one next year!" as she pointed to all of us. Yes, she was pregnant with my Cousin Janet. Now Janet is married with three adult sons over eighteen years old.

Aunt Muriel came next. My Aunt Muriel and Mother are so much alike that they could be thought of as twins. She is very orderly and tidy to this very day with white, starched sheets covering furniture and rugs. She married my Uncle Jackie (now deceased) in her late teens. Uncle Jackie laughed and joked around a lot, especially on the summer weekends when he and the other fathers used to drive down to the Cape to see us all. Little did I realize at the time that my uncle had a drinking problem for years. It was not until my Cousin Jay was born in the 1960's with Down's syndrome that my Uncle stopped drinking completely. He internally blamed himself, but if this stopped him from drinking, it was God's motivation

It was when I got older that I really got to know my Uncle Jackie. My Uncle Jackie used to do a lot with my Cousin Jay and me like bringing us to various events like Willie Nelson concerts on Boston Commons. I recall in particular Saturday nights when my Mom, Dad and I visited my Uncle Jack and Aunt Muriel either up the project in Everett or their house in Saugus for a delicious spaghetti dinner, with my Cousin Jay playing Country and Western music until the wee hours of Sunday's mornings. And game after game of beating my uncle at Scrabble. Those were the days I shall never erase from my memory, because all the family used to be together.

And, of course, there was the trip to California I will particularly never, never forget the terrifying ride down the steep and narrow road from Yosemite National Park in our rented station wagon with eight of us including uncles, aunts and cousins just praying that he would not go off the path. Uncle Jackie's driving skills were very debatable.

Aunt Muriel and Uncle Jackie had two older children who are now around sixty and fifty-five. Their names are Johnny and Joyce and presently all four of them are still living in California.

Aunt Joyce went in the service prior to marrying my Uncle Jeff who is now deceased. I never liked my Uncle Jeff when I knew him as a little girl, but I could not explain why to my Mother. My Mother could not understand until time went on when finding out he used to be very overbearing and abusive to my aunt both psychologically and physically. It seemed my Uncle Jeff was the monarch of the whole household and a very insecure human being as I found out when I got older. He told my aunt what to wear, how to get to work each day (while he followed her) and when she could see her relatives. Thinking back, who knew what else went on behind closed doors with my four cousins? I will always recall as the years passed my Mom looking at me saying "You were right all those years."

Otherwise, my Auntie Joyce was a very smart woman. I understand she was a supervisor of some big company with girls under her.

Her four children were Tommy, Wayne, and Scott and Debbie. In reality, I think her life was quite a tragic one, not only in her marriage, but two of her sons passed away years ago and the remaining two have heart and stroke problems.

Finally there is my Uncle Gordon who resides down Cape Cod. Last year my Aunt Diane died of cancer leaving three adult children: Marie, Cathy and Gordon.

Chapter Two

My Youth

My brother, Frank Thomas Sanfilippo, was born thirteen months after me on June 7, 1954 and my sister, Nancy, on August 27, 1956.

My brother, Frank, was named after my Grandfather Sanfilippo and Grandfather Campbell as Frank Thomas. He weighed in at over ten pounds when he was born, and by nine months he was already walking and climbing out of his crib which had my Mother running in circles as she was taking care of my daily living needs at the same time. She was not used to having a child running around or getting out of a crib at nine months old.

When my sister Nancy was small she looked like a doll with curly, blond hair. She was a very quiet little girl. At the early age of twenty-one my sister got married. Before my sister's children came along, she worked at Deaconess Hospital in Boston as a secretary in the cancer department and after her second child was born she stayed home with her children days and worked a few nights as a bartender after her husband got home from work. She had two children by her first husband, a boy Daniel and a girl Lindy.

It was extremely difficult for my Mother to have three of us in diapers, but two children getting into everything as children are apt to do and one who could not even pick up a simple spoon. In days to come I compensated for some of my inabilities. Without being able to use my hands, I used to compensate by using my nose to play my small table electric organ, Nana Campbell's piano and turn pages of a book. I can say proudly that I played the organ very well. A couple of my favorite tunes were "Mary had a Little Lamb" And "Jingle Bells" which I have to admit I played pretty well. Maybe I should have had became a great pianist! ! !

From then on my Mother was a stay at home mom and took a lot of pride in raising my brother, Frank, my sister Nancy and me. We were all in diapers and my mom had her hands full, with caring for me or overlooking me while I was rolling along in my walker, while at the same time worrying what my brother Frankie was up to. He was a real typical little boy running around the house and teasing or egging on my sister constantly like most brothers do. At that time, when my mother had to go chase and look after my brother's own safety and welfare, I experienced how it felt when she let go of me and placed me in my highchair. I felt my arms and my legs as being useless and what would happen if I fell out of my chair? I did have a walker for a short time but after a few falls I never wanted to see that walker again. Although it was only moments before my mother returned and picked me up again, the feeling of abandonment came like a giant wave over me and left me paralyzed with terror. I was always in my mother's or father's arms and when they could not carry me my aunts and my uncles were there. I know my brother suffered severely from having a sister who was disabled because my mom often took her frustrations out on him. He was simply a healthy little boy with a lot of energy and sometimes my mother became overwhelmed and took it out on him by hitting him. As I think back, Frankie took a lot of abuse, which if it was in this day and age, it would have been dealt with differently by social workers and the state.

Although my father loved all of his children so deeply and clearly, there was one thing which especially troubled me and that was the way he designed different apparatuses for me to sit in wherever we went out in public so people would not gawk at me. It took years before he finally resigned himself to the reality that I needed a wheelchair. The very first chair he made for me was no ordinary high chair! He made me a really fancy highchair with a tray attached to it along with four sides. I felt like I was sitting in the middle of my very own personal dining table with the center cut out where my comfy chair was. It was situated in our kitchen where most of the activity of family life happened.

The second piece of apparatus he found for me was , believe it or not, a shopping cart. I do not know what store parking lot he got it from but I do remember him pushing it with me in it. Talk about not attracting attention! I would have been better off in a stroller, and he would probably have not gotten the looks he got from the neighbors or the public.

Finally after many long and tiring trips to The Children's Hospital and Massachusetts General in Boston for physical, occupational and speech therapies, both my parents had to come to the realization that in order to support my body so that I had some measure of comfort my own personally built wheelchair was needed. Also, it was at this point of time that they were confronted by social workers and speech and physical therapists. Along with this, I was tested over and over on my mental capability. Was I slow as so many were who had Cerebral Palsy?

This question was answered after so many various tests with different shapes and colored blocks and puzzles. I was very frustrated at times while doing these tests because I had little hand coordination and was therefore not able to put puzzle parts together. During these times, I wondered why I had to do this. It was at these periods that I felt it so unfair because all I wanted was to play with my cousins and siblings. It was at these times, too, that I felt like I was in a circus side show, when interns and other specialists gawked at me. In truth I never really got used to it because they knew so little about Cerebral Palsy, which affected each child in a different way both physically and mentally. It was caused by the lack of oxygen at birth (which was in my case), alcohol consumption during pregnancy or by a head trauma later in life. Finally, at the age of five all of the so-called experts at Mass. General Hospital informed my parents that their little girl was very bright but would become very frustrated because she would not be able to do anything due to her physical condition. Oh boy! They were all so wrong!

Apart from these horrifying days, I had a fairly "normal" upbringing. Summers were spent (when we weren't down Cape Cod either staying at rented cottages of my Grandparents Campbell or my Uncle Gordon's home in South Yarmouth) driving around either in a small red Volkswagen bug, a Chevy station wagon with and numerous of other automobiles which my Dad owned. I just recall my Mom, my sister, brother and I use to drive for hours every week. I can say the car was a second home to me because we went out in it almost every day for short trips. My Dad would take us along the Boulevard on Revere Beach which was formerly well-known as Crescent Beach, the nation's first public beach in 1896, where they had a roller coaster stretching three thousand and six hundred feet of track that traveled at the speed of fifty mile per hour and a merry-go-around which I always got ill on whenever I went on it when my Aunt Lilly and Uncle Sonny took me often. We would stop for pizza at a place called Anna's Pizza or Bianchi's, or get a fried fish plate at Kelly's Roast Beef joint where the cost was only fifty cents then. My Mom's sanity was kept in check by my Dad's excursions to

Marblehead to see how the wealthy lived in their big mansions and castles situated overlooking Marblehead Bay and yacht club. I can honestly say the car was my second home. Although I have to say my Dad's driving left a lot to be desired at times. He used to drive up other peoples' behind, which drove my Mom absolutely crazy. I'm actually surprised that there was never a hole in the floor on the front passenger's side where my Mom usually sat! One time all three of us, Dad, Mother and I, almost got killed after they picked me up from college. My Dad thought he saw a wallet in the road and went back for it. While we were stopped, another car drove right into the back of my van, slamming my two hundred pound motorized wheelchair with me belted in it all the way to the back of the van, while my Mother was caught in the front seat and my Dad's seat was literally in the lying position. Yes, he was a bad driver…

When we did not venture on those car outings my sister and I played out on the side of the house. We had a big, long driveway to play on with my cousins Kathy, Terry (who were like sisters to me) and neighborhood kids enjoyed in challenging games such as Red Light, Simon Says, Hide and Go Seek, and Barbies for hours on end. Although I could not use my hands to pick-up the dolls, either Nancy, Kathy or Terry held them up for me while we played. When we got old enough to be allowed off of the street, Kathy and I ventured to the corner drug store to buy bubble gum, Hershey candy bars or a Hoodsie ice cream cup of vanilla and chocolate. Oh, how free we felt at those times. There were a couple of times Kathy played hooky from school and we went across Nichols Street to the Hamilton Elementary School and stood outside of my sister's classroom to get her attention. As you can probably guess, this got my sister and the rest of the students in deep trouble because they ended up standing on their desk chairs trying to see us. From this experience, I became the class Victorian and invited to come to class one afternoon. Soon my adventures with my Cousin Kathy came to an abrupt ending. I can still commit to memory when Kathy came upon her teenaged years and she just disappeared from my life while my Cousin Terry, who was four years younger than I, started hanging around with me. We would sit at the kitchen table and raid my parents' refrigerator of olives, cheese, pickles and hot cherry peppers. AND, OF COURSE, Terry's wonderful strong iced coffee. What a terrible combination, don't you think?! But, it was SO good! Let me say, too, there were at times backlashes for our indulgence hours later. Indigestion and heartburn kicked in often with air coming from both ends!

I especially remember when I was in my teens my Dad purchased a second hand red motor scooter. We rode on the school grounds across the street from the house during the weekends. My Mom still has regrets about letting me go on while my brother or sister held me. All I recollect is the complete freedom that I felt on the scooter - like being able to walk or fly!

During the winters I went out sledding or just sat in the snow which was at least two feet deep watching the rest of the neighborhood kids building snowmen with two heads. My favorite activity was sled rides in the middle of our street where someone pulled me down the empty, icy terrain for hours on end.

My Christmases were such exciting and happy times for me back when I was a child prior to coming to the truth that Santa never existed. (I wondered why my parents stayed up half of the night!!!) . Since I can remember, we always had gigantic, real Christmas trees decorated with bright colored ornaments and silver garland (always a strand of it used to turn up somehow months later somewhere in the house) which were purchased mostly at Filene's Basement (my mother's favorite store!). The one thing I wish not to commit to memory was when my parents put up the trees each year! What a hassle it was placing the tree trunk in the narrow stands and in those days when one light bulb blew the entire string of lights did too! It was at these particular times that I saw my Dad's distaste for this holiday in particular, saying "You kids are spoiled brats, etc., etc! I never had a tree." In the long run, he spoiled us every year. Each year I woke up at the crack of dawn on Christmas morning and just knew that my brother and sister were lying in their beds, wide awake and full of anticipation too. We woke up so early that my Mother had to tell us to go back to bed for an hour. When we were finally allowed to get up, Frankie and Nancy would go straight for their stockings like magnets to steel. They were filled with candy canes and chocolate Santas. My dad got me up with the others by making no haste to my room where he put his arms around me and lifted me out of bed, carrying me into our brightly lit living room while I laughed and wiggled around in his arms. Our stockings were hung on the mantle in the hallway which led into the living room. By this time Nancy and Frankie were well into their stockings, I, too, was so excited to see what Santa had delivered the night before. Under our beautifully lit Christmas tree, gifts were stacked as high as the bottom branches and came spilling out onto the living room rug. I especially remember two

Christmas's mornings back in the mid fifties and sixties when I got a walking doll. I wonder if any readers remember the movie, "The Bride of Chucky?" Well, one year that same doll {or so I thought} was under the tree with my name on it! My mother was fiddling with a part on a life size doll and next thing I know this foreboding doll with curly brown hair and apple red cheeks started to talk and walk towards me. I don't know why, but I started to feel my heart race in fear. I let out such a wail that I must have shocked my mother. I am certain she wasn't expecting me to react like that. Craziest thing was, my sister and brother were afraid of the doll too. Oh yea, the doll named Winnie was and still is the scariest doll I ever had the pleasure to be gifted with! I found out she still resides in my old bedroom at my mother's home, lying in wait, just staring at the door ready to get out of her chair and talk and walk to me.

Another Christmas in the mid 1960's I got my first method of communication , an electric IBM typewriter which I operated with my head stick. Little did I know then how important this little piece of wood attached to an elastic band with a six inch stick protruding from of it would make me so independent in my education endeavors and my communication skills.

And, how could I forget my children's rocking chair and first record player. How I drove my mom and dad wild rocking back and forth in that chair, because I was able to rock back and forth all by myself using only my legs to propel me forward and back while rocking back and forth to the beat to my Beatles' albums. I keep in mind these Christmas gifts had been put in the kitchen instead of under the tree, so I wouldn't see them right away. My mother feigned ignorance when she saw the boxes and asked me, "What are these parcels?" When she took off their covers and I saw what it was I was thrilled. I believe in time my parents regretted giving me that record player because I constantly played Beatles records over and over. I even had the bedroom changed when my brother Frank got his own room into a Beatles Museum with four huge, white, framed posters that my Dad made for me on the wall of Paul, George, John and Ringo. We were all spoiled on the holidays.

My father's siblings lived upstairs for quite awhile and because he was the oldest of his five brothers and two sisters I was like their little sister, because of the small age difference. They were all so good to me and I was always given a lot of attention.

21

This was especially true of my Uncle Frank, Jr, (ten year older than I) whom I call Uncle Junior, which he didn't like one bit and the older he got the more he disliked it. He called me "Pickle". He was like a big brother to me. It was during this time, when I was about four and a half years old , that I started kindergarten for children with Cerebral Palsy, which was held somewhere in Wellesley, Massachusetts for some months and then moved to The Children's Hospital in Boston. It was there that I learned how to really talk, read, add and subtract, but it was Uncle Junior who showed me how to move the muscles in my mouth, and so my pronunciation improved greatly. He also taught me how to use a straw to drink with, which was probably one of the most important lessons in my life for me, a matter of survival. Little did anyone know that I did not have the ability to suck on the bottle all during infancy, so I was hungry the majority of the time and my Mom told me that when I finally got the knack of how to suck the bottle I went to town on finishing my milk because I was so hungry. She even had to place a big sheet in front of me since I tended to spit it all up again. I believe they all must have had the patience of saints. Both my parents and relatives helped me so much in dealing with the everyday struggles of my youth .

During the fifties the style of interior design was much different than today so everything in our apartment would have been considered modern and right in style with the times. The kitchen was tiled halfway up the walls and had a bit of maroon color enlacing it. My mother chose to hang blue and white wallpaper on the top half of the walls because blue was and still is her favorite color. Oh, boy. What a combination! The floor was tiled with maroon and off- white big huge squares. The two bedrooms were separated by a long hallway which was carpeted with an orange shag wall to wall rug. Our bedroom consisted of a twin bed for my brother and a full sized bed for my sister and me which we shared until we became too old to. Our living room was where my brother, sister and I gathered Mondays through Fridays mornings to watch Captain Kangaroo and Romper Room with Miss Jean in the hopes she would mention our names while she looked through her looking glass. It was not until we were well into our teens, when unfortunately, my mother let my brother take over in the living room as he started dating. We had a light oak console television, radio and record player which were all in that room. A large sectional couch was up against a really ugly, dark paneled wall. My mother had good taste in interior design so she made the most of what she had to work with and afford.

On my Mother's side of the family I grew up like any other grandchild, although looking back, both sides were very different. My Grandpa Campbell, a very distinguished looking man with a full head of thick, curly, pallid hair, was a proof reader and ran newspaper presses in Boston, so at the time he was considered well off. My Mother said they had the first automobile on their street.

For about fifty years they resided on Reed Avenue in Everett until 1972. We went to their house mainly for birthday parties, holidays and occasional Sunday dinners. During these infrequent Sunday's dinners of lamb or beef, with numerous side dishes of vegetables and, of course, potatoes, I still bear in mind the plates had to be warm when my Nana Campbell served these meals. The one most irritating thing was my Grandmother's cuckoo clock which drove me insane when it went off every fifteen minutes. Little did I know that I would inherit it in decades to come! The best time came after we, the grandchildren, were formally excused from the dinner table to venture downstairs to my Grandpa's secret amusement park inside a huge cellar where my Grandfather had built a whole city of trains. It was remarkable and entertained all of us when we visited. There were small figures like trees, sidewalks, houses with train tracks going through cities and towns. It was quite amazing. The dreadful reality came when he had enough of our noise and when we had to leave to go home.

All I remembered about my Grandfather Campbell was that he was a quiet man and a strict Baptist. He did not like children, although he had five. His belief was children should be seen but not heard from. All I remember was whenever we were all in his presence the children had to be soundless diminutive robots as my Mother was continuously whispering "Be quiet" to my brother and sister. I, myself, even disliked my Grandfather as a young girl. I also can still hear him calling me "What a spoiled brat" because my Mother could not be out of my sight or I used to scream. Little did he realize that my Mother was my legs and arms from the physical imprisonment I was in. As I grew into my teens, I came to terms that there was this brash air about him like the world revolved around him and no one else. This was the truth I found out as I discovered his infidelity with other women during his marriage with my Grandmother. When I got much older and wiser, I came to the realization that my grandfather, like many other people, just played the role of a true Christian. If he was a so-called Christian, he would not have cheated on my Grandmother or needed to preach the Bible when he came over for visits ,reading it for hours and not being able to just say "Hi, Gail" to his granddaughter. I felt his discomfort when in my presence. For a so called Christian, he was the worst example I have ever seen.

After my Grandpa Campbell died in his sleep in 1972 of natural causes, my Grandmother began staying at my aunt's house and our house for a few days each week. It was during these years I really got to know her. She was always happy with a great sense of humor. She used to putter around the house watching my Dad cook, always asking questions about how he made whatever he made. My Dad always joked with her trying to hide his recipes. At this time, I was in high school or college so from my bedroom I could always hear laughter and wondered what the two of them were up to. She had this funny habit I guess that came with getting up in years. Spontaneously and uncontrollably my Nana, as she walked she used to just let out wind. I guess things do become more unmanageable when the years go by because now at times I spontaneously let out wind!

During the next remaining twelve years of my Grandmother Campbell's life she taught me so much. She was always encouraging me and said how I was able to do whatever I wanted despite my disability. She was so right. When she passed away in late April of 1984, a couple days before her 90th birthday and after an operation on her hip, I realized I did not only lose a grandmother but a best friend as well.

My Mom who had no idea as to whether I was able to control my bladder had a big surprise when she just put me on the toilet one day. I can still hear my Mom calling my father by his nickname "Iggie, Gail went pee on the toilet!" I guess this was a big revelation to my parents, but at the time, I wondered what the big hullabaloo was all about. As I sat on my sister's yellow duck toilet in the middle of this excitement, I really did not know what I did that was so right. I guess I did something special, because it was broadcasted all through the four family house that we lived in half of my life! I guess it decreased the number of diapers my Mother had to wash!

My Mother was the authoritarian parent. When we did something wrong or acted up, all we had to do was to look at her and we knew we were in trouble. Her eyes said a lot. She did not even need to open her mouth. The anger showed in her big blue eyes so vividly and intensely. I also recollect she was constantly doing housework even when we were out just in the driveway with next door neighbors, cousins and my Nana San. Looking back, I see this was her whole existence: being a mother, wife and housekeeper. There was a rumor or a joke going around the neighborhood that she had to be taking in other peoples' laundry because the clothes lines were always full. She was a perfectionist. Everything had to look just right, including us kids. Even when we went out to just play, both my sister and I wore fancy dresses. I was relentlessly asked if I was going to a party by neighbors. Just imagine playing hide and go seek, red light and hopscotch in a fancy, frilly dress ! It just did not quite work. Sometimes I felt this perfectionism came somewhat from a desire to hide the imperfections of me. With everything looking just right on the outside, I think it made my Mother feel whole on the inside.

Chapter Three

My Education

There were a lot of things that people guessed wrong about me. I did not die after birth as they said I was supposed to, so why should I believe the "fact" that I couldn't go to school? So at the age of five I started on my way to kindergarten for a short time in Wellesley, Massachusetts and onto Children Hospital in Boston , which had special programs for children between the ages of four and eight years old with Cerebral Palsy. I hated it whenever I went. I cried every day my parents dropped me off anywhere. The first day of so-called kindergarten I faced this middle aged woman who was the head teacher, a Miss Maloney. My first impression of her was that of the wicked witch in the classic movie "Wizard of Oz." I can still perceive her in my psyche as a plump, unyielding witch of the West. Even at the young age of five or six I could tell she detested her job immensely just by the way she treated us. In truth, I believe now she hated herself. She had an attitude like she was angry at the whole world and she took it out on us. Reflecting back on her now, she could be as nasty as she could be nice . Maybe she was going through the change of life or the need of a man's arms around her but whatever her life may had been, she took all of her frustrations out on us kids. Why not? We were only cripples at her mercy.

There was another teacher that I remember very clearly. Mrs. Loyde taught me the alphabet and how to read . The first book I read from was "Dick and Jane." This teacher was a striking , very kind and soft spoken individual . Perhaps that was because she had a daughter who had Cerebral Palsy too, but with many more disabilities than myself. The daughter , Joan, was older and sat in high back wheelchair which supported her head and I remember that she communicated only by moaning and making grunting noises.

Unlike Miss Maloney who was overweight, Miss Lane was a frail lady who was the physical therapist. I do not think she had a life outside of Children's Hospital. She always looked old to me, maybe because she acted the part.

She was not a blissful individual and she didn't seem to take much pleasure in her work , which was reflected in her bad attitude towards us kids. She was either yelling or instructing us how we should do our exercises the correct way. Maybe her main purpose in this world was to torture the cripples by stretching our spastic limbs. I know she was only doing her job, but it was the way she talked and yelled at us at the same time which still puzzles me. By today's standards it would be called verbal abuse.

At about eight and a half, I went away from home to Crotched Mountain Rehabilitation Center in Greenfield, New Hampshire during two time periods which added up to four-teen months in all between 1961-1963.

I thought the nightmare started the first time I was left there, but I was wrong. When I was seated in my small wheelchair in the library while my parents suddenly vanished from my sight, it felt like my parents were deserting me, giving me up for dead. It was at this time that I felt suddenly and totally all alone. It seemed I wept for hours and days.

The next couple of days, which seemed like months, were filled with blended liquid meals always in different shades of green and enemas day after day when I did not shit. I could eat solid food and shit every other day or so, but the nurse's aides never listened to me or contacted my parents for days on end. As for the enemas, I almost was given one every day in front of the other girls in this big, open spaced bathroom with only three private stalls. The rest of the bathroom consisted of two lines of small toilet seats without any solitude whatsoever. This was just one method used to take away our dignity. As each day overlapped into another, I pleaded and sobbed to the nurse's aides to call my mother to find out my eating and toileting habits, but the call wasn't made for days.

I remember my Dad and Mom driving me back to school every other Sunday evening after my Dad got out of work at eleven pm from General Electric. The route was always the same: Burlington, Massachusetts (Route 93) to Route 3 toward New Hampshire.

As my father made this turn, I knew I was on my way back to the daily enema injections and the lack of any privacy. Oh, how I loathed going back to school after these weekends with my family and literally cried and protested all the way there. Every other weekend when I could not go home, my Dad and Mom used to drive three hours all the way to the school just to take me out. My favorite spot was a tiny pond down the hilly road from the school where at times my brother went ice fishing or skating. I was wheeled on the icy surface in my wheelchair, praying the whole time that it was cold enough so my wheelchair and I would not fall through!

Most of the time, my brother and sister stayed home with relatives. Looking back now at my life forty-three years ago, I realize more clearly what my parents sacrificed and went through for me: Everything! Sometimes I think about if this affected my brother and sister. Of course, it had to in some way. Sometimes guilt creeps through my veins but , on the other hand, it wasn't my fault being disabled. There was not anyone or anything to blame but fate and destiny we cannot control.

Crotched Mountain Rehabilitation Center was a rehabilitation facility mainly for disabled and deaf people. It basically provided education and physical therapy programs starting in the 1940's. In 1948 it opened its forty room Children's Center, which served children with Polio. In 1954 it opened up a building for educational and community activities, which expanded into a school for deaf. Its growth continued into the late 1950's and early 1960's as it offered expanded vocational and residential services.

The primary objective of CMRC was to try to find the full potential of patients and then kick them out into the real world. This was perfectly fine but in the real world individuals do not get an enema everyday if one does not take a shit, eat blended food, go to bed right at eight o'clock each night or be restricted to only going home every other weekend. I can still recall the smell of the place and how it was laid out. As you walked in from the front entrance to the right was an auditorium where we put on plays and to the left was a corridor that headed to hell. Down this corridor were all the classrooms and areas for Speech, Occupational and Physical Therapies and Psychiatrists who hovered over each client daily, trying to put each of us into a category. Down this corridor were people of the three professions working together to see what a client could or could not do. They had made accurate evaluations regarding me as I read in my records today. I was very competitive then as I am today. As for my social skills, I have always wanted to be involved with my fellow students as well as the nurse aides and staff. Yes, I was and still am a social butterfly!

In the Physical Therapy Department they had me in a full body brace that extended up to my armpits and down to my feet and I was walking with crutches. It was great, but they finally came to the conclusion that I had little control over my arms so if I chose to continue this path I would always need someone standing behind me. What was the sense of this?

Speech Therapy consisted of blowing bubbles and enunciating the sounds of the letters of the alphabet. I also did breathing and swallowing exercises.

Occupational Therapy was trying to experience what I could do with my hands. One day they strapped a spoon in my right hand to see if I could feed myself. It was a miracle I did not poke my eyes out!

The right side of the corridor contained our hell of discipline and behavior, the dormitories. This area was where secrets were never revealed or talked about. I swear the devils were sent here by God to torture us mentally and physically, but who could prove it? It was only our word against the nurses' aides. There was a time that I slept right under this big window that had no drapes. There was a view of the outside walkway right where people walked to and from the girls' and boys' dorms. Between the fear of someone walking along the walkway peeping his head in the window and the terrible, loud thunderstorms, I used to be so afraid that I usually slept with the bed covers over my head just listening to all of the creaks in the floor and in the walls around me.

Picture this- It was the middle of the night, the air inside the dorm where I slept was heavy and foreboding. The huge window under which I slept was barren of any protection . With no drapes on the windows, the sound of the rain drops seemed like someone was tapping his fingertips on the windowpane trying to come in. Someone from the outside trying to bring in the evils of the world, but little did he know he was entering into a different hell, a hell I came to know very well over the fourteen month period of rehabilitation at Crotched Mountain Center.

As sand little by little trickles down in an hourglass, so did my days go by in the first couple of months at Crotched Mountain. Days began at the break of dawn when, in the distance, I heard the shoes of the graveyard shift nurse clicking on the bare, cold, tiled floor. While she strolled her way toward the ten bed dormitory, she would start the sour day by only a switch of a button which ignited the fluorescent glare. "Good morning, girls!" she said as she danced her way around to each of our beds, dragging the bedding off. When she came my way, I said "I can't get dressed by myself, so let me sleep until the seven to three o'clock shift comes on." Ninety-five percent of the time she just walked away, but the other five percent, my covers were snatched off and she woke me up anyway. As I laid there for two hours, I would contemplate who I was assigned to for the day. Would it be the old maid with the starched, crisp white nurse's cap who hit me because she could never get my brace shoes on due to my spasticity? Or the one dressed in her blue uniform, white nylons and shoes who put me in a crib one night because I just asked if I could stay up fifteen minutes longer? A nurse's aide, named Donna Hazel, had a great influence on me. Hazel, as we all called her, was of big stature, blond, and about fourteen years older than myself and took a liking towards me. She frequently took me upstairs to the nurse aides' quarters or drove me home to Everett with her brother, Bucky, who I instantly had a crush on with his little boyish face and flaxen, wavy hair. I even recall songs which were out at that time: "Puff, The Magic Dragon" and "Bobby's Girl" originally sung by Marcie Blane, played over and over on the car radio. Of course, each time "Bobby's Girl" came blaring over the air waves, Hazel always changed the lyrics to "Bucky's Girl!" teasing me ritually. But there was a dark side to Hazel that I saw in the months to come. I saw on one particular night that she could be as nice as she was cruel. When I asked if I could stay up fifteen minutes past my bedtime, it was then that she had to get the "control" back into her own restricted life from the extremely restricted environment she lived in her living quarters upstairs. Now I realize looking back that maybe Hazel's life might had been as restricted as our own. Hazel was the one who put me in the baby's crib.

At seven o'clock each and every morning I knew my fate for the next eight hours at least. Good or bad, I had no choice or say in the matter.

First the day began with the struggle of putting on my leg braces. Just putting on the stiff shoes took ten minutes and this was because I was usually so spastic. This task alone took an aide from 7:15 to 7:20 AM. Then the corset which resembled the girdles women wore back in the eighteen hundreds had to be laced up. This took about five to seven minutes. Next was my favorite activity of the day: "the bathroom," to wash up, pee and, of course, an enema if needed.

On to the dining room we would go, wheeling by the elevator where the nurses go to their own living quarters, turning right, passing the library and left to the cafeteria where we were either introduced to cold cereal or lumpy oatmeal. At one side sat the boys and girls from the deaf school that was located downstairs. I recall fondly how I made them laugh making faces over the food we were given.

The grueling day really embarked on us at nine o'clock and continued until four or five o'clock , five days a week, month after month. Between hours in the classroom and all of the therapies where our limbs were either being stretched on the floor and our vocal cords or tongues being exercised by blowing bubbles and licking peanut butter from the roof of our mouths, the days were full and exhausting. In between, we had a so-called rest period with some of us laying on our bed with our leg braces locked to stretch out our knee ligaments. When rest period was through, it started all over again, schooling or a therapy of some sort .

Finally the minutes rolled around to nights, which were the scariest part of my day, when the enemas were routinely stuck up the rectums of many who did not shit on their own during the hectic day.

By the time we all got out of Crotched Mountain, I believe we were much stronger individuals in mind and spirit. It was an institution despite the fact that I learned how to type with a head stick which freed my body and mind.

It was here I began the lessons of my religious beliefs of the Catholic Religion. A young woman named Carol, who was an Occupational Therapist and planning to go into the nunnery, taught lessons for First Holy Communion. I do not memorize much of it now, but I do remember the most primary and important prayers we had to know. I can still see myself on that day wearing a white lace dress with a veil on my head. I looked like an angel. Or a crippled angel with leg braces that kept me from moving. I can still recall years later that when I went to confessions I had this thin book which illustrated the major sins that a ten to fifteen year old could commit . I used my head stick to point to the sins so that the Priest could understand what I had done.

On Tuesday, August 14, 2007 I got enough courage to revisit my school and my demons.

Prior to this psychological journey into my past, I got in contact with this man, Tracy Messer, who is a Marketing Manager up at Crotched. As soon as he heard I was an alumnus of the place his enthusiasm blossomed, but not for very long. After a few emails between the two of us, the air was thick and steamy.

Dear Mr. Messer,

I would like to make it another day soon, because this is going to be research for my book. Although Crotched Mountain may be a wonderful place now, forty-five years ago it terrorized me as a nine year old child and STILL does.

Thank you for the day you have planned for me and I'll be looking forward to hearing from you.

Keep in touch,

Gail Sanfilippo

Dear Mr. Messer:

How come you can't write back? Don't know the right words to say?

Well, this was 95% of my "reality" in Crotched Mountain. It isn't any of your fault, but you need to know. I was only a nine year old little girl, too.

Sincerely,

Gail Sanfilippo

Dear Mr. Messer:

After reading your email, you need to know A LOT of my "reality" while I was in C.M. You need to realize too that you only work there five days a week for forty hours a week in your own nice, cozy office away from the dorms, etc.

1. Daily enemas if one didn't take a shit each day.

2. Windows without drapes/curtains while terrible thunderstorms and lightening light the whole dorm rooms.

3. Wakeup at 5:00 am, while many of us needed assistance at 7:00 am when the first shift came on duty.

4. Being hit by an aid, because one is spastic when she is yelling at me, because she is unable to put my brace shoes on.

5. Being put in a baby crib when asked if I could stay up fifteen minutes after schedule.

6. Not allowed to go home each weekend.

Do you wish me to go on, Mr. Messer? ? ?

Gail Sanfilippo

Entering the town of Wilton, New Hampshire we stopped for gas. As my partner and part-time PCA, Ed, was in the bathroom, I just sat in the car observing the people around me. They talked and acted as if they were characters in old slow motion movies from decades ago. Life was so different up here it seemed. If something did not get done that day, there was time tomorrow, next week or next month.

When we were on the road again we had to take a detour through the town due to construction work going on right in the middle of town. This was another adventure driving through the narrow and winding streets of Wilton. On each lot of land houses were unique in and of themselves like match-box houses on Hampton Beach or Plum Island.

After maneuvering in and out these streets, the main road became two lanes. It was here I realized how my parents sacrificed so much for their daughter. Just traveling up to the place in the light of day on endless, winding roads was terrifying; never mind in the shadows of night. As Ed drove, I could feel my body getting spastic and my stomach rolling. The Kaeopectate which I had taken three hours earlier could not quit now! Looking out at the scenery, I realized how small I was in this vast world, like an ant just trying to survive each and everyday we are given on this earth. Finally I saw familiar surroundings, the small pond where my brother loved to ice fish and the rest of us used to freeze our behinds off in the middle of winter. Now it looked so different. The pond looked so much smaller then I imagined it was forty-five years ago. Everything looked different, or was it that I erased so much from my memory? Along the mountainous and curves in the road there seemed to be more dwellings built. If I did not know any better, I would have thought I was taking a ride in the wilderness of Maine where individuals were either poor or affluent.

As we droved towards Greenfield, my ears became blocked. I said in my mind "Was this a sign by the devil telling me not to go up there? Going to the place of shear hell for an eight and a half year old little girl who couldn't stick up for herself due to garbled speech and physical limitations which she was given accidentally at birth? Was this why I think many individuals had taken advantage of me throughout my life? Well, if this was the truth, it was going to come to an end today.

Then around the corner there it was! The big sign that looked like a billboard loomed right in front of me indicating the entrance into my years of hell past, a bold , navy blue and gold sign in the ground with the lettering of "Crotched Mountain Educational and Rehabilitation Center." I thought to myself right away "At least they made an improve-ment at the gateway from reality into hell." After that thought, the car came to a standstill as Ed suddenly pulled over and stepped out to become photographer of the day as he hiked up the road six yards from the car taking numerous photos of the sign and God knows what. He gestured an impulsive wave towards me which I thought was a nod of a "Hi!" but, to my surprise there was a deer crossing the road approximately six yards away from the back of the car. Of course, I missed it, for two rational reasons: we were invading his territory and I do not have the ability of swirling my neck around like Linda Blair in the movie "Exorcist!" The butterflies came back to my stomach as soon as Ed started the car and turned right at the sign. As we drove toward the main building the view was out of this world . There were diverse shapes and tones of green peaks and valleys everywhere in the distance as far as the eye could see. I reflected on the contrast between this scenery and the buildings which were on this mountain. I tried to keep my face as tranquil as possible but there it was: my hell. It all came over me like a tidal wave racing after me and I could not run from it anymore. As the car turned into the parking lot I could see that the main building had had some renovations done on the outside. There were brightly painted colors like the entrance sign, but what scared the shit out of me was on the other side. When I heard the van's lockdowns being released I started becoming numb. I tried to hide my inner anxiety from Ed by talking about how different and more cheerful the exterior was. Inside I was dying and just wanted to run. Apparently it worked because Ed only asked me what door to go in. "The first door, cause that's the auditorium." I suddenly felt his eyes looking down at me as if to say "You remember?" I believe we went through the entrance where the doors opened automatically. I actually can not remember as we came across a receptionist desk. As we waited for this woman, who had to be in her late fifties or early sixties, to get off the telephone I took inventory of my surroundings. So much had changed. The long, cold, beige, tiled corridor to the dormitories and offices for social workers was replaced with big glassed windows and brightly painted walls. I had to see the auditorium! It was still there but they took all of the auditorium seats out and replaced them with long tables with red backed folding chairs. It actually looked a gym with bare, wooden floors or a game room where patients or residents could play cards or hold meetings.

By this time the receptionist was off the phone and wondering where we went. When we reached the desk, she immediately tried to get in contact with Mr. Messer, whom I really did not care to see, but she obviously did not know about our emails back and forth. Thankfully, he could not be reached. I think he too did not want any contact with me. Finally she said "He must be in the cafeteria with another visitor, so feel free to go there," gesturing the directions with her right hand. I told her: "I think I remember" in which she stared at me in the most bizarre way. After asking Ed to tell her that I had been a client forty-five years ago, I wondered if she knew how much psychological torture I was in that day. Of course, she thought it was so wonderful to see alumni up to visit.

Wheeling to the cafeteria really brought back a stream of memories and emotions in me. I was rolling toward my "real" hell: the dormitory and the library where about forty-six years ago I felt I had been forsaken. Now it was so different. They had turned it into a unit for people who got brain injured during their later years. I had to go through this glass door to get rid of seventy-five percent of my evil spirits, but Ed noticed they had the door locked which could only be entered with security cards. So, with this obstacle in the way Ed automatically wheeled me away from the crime scene in the direction of the cafeteria, thinking to himself: "Thank you, Jesus!" He did not know that along the way there was "the library." As he wheeled me I saw it was no longer there. I guessed I had an eerie look on my face. They turned "the library" into conference and meeting rooms with long tables and nice, upholstered office chairs. I wondered what they discussed behind these doors, but deep down in my heart I knew. They were either discussing how to receive funding or a client's condition and potential.

I found out my patient profile during this past summer when they released all my records to me. I am described as "involved, competitive, although she is very disabled physically and has a problem communicating with others she does not know or know her..." . I guess they taught me how to really communicate by teaching me how to type with a head stick, because I have come a long way since. I can even say "Fuck" which everyone regretfully understands whenever it comes out of my mouth in a fit of anger or laughter! The looks and the reactions I get are so funny. Either people view me as being truly retarded or just laugh with me knowing I am right in my reaction to the situation. I think that they wish they could get away with it too.

We soon made it to the cafeteria by turning left at the end of the corridor. Of course, there was no sign of Mr. Messer waiting for me which was not a surprise. He probably went into hiding as soon as the front desk receptionist first talked to him a half hour ago. As Ed tried to get a bite of lunch, we were confronted by a cashier in her late fifties speaking in a sarcastic and abrupt tone, telling us "The cafeteria is closing in three minutes!" It was all I could do not to lash out at her saying "Who do you think you're talking to?

We aren't patients here who you can dump your anger or frustration on," but Ed wheeled me just in time, asking me what did I want to see before we left? In my mind, I knew I had to go back down the hall to see the dormitory to set my mind at peace, so we went. The door was open so Ed controlled my chair through the opened door and there I was, seeing that ninety percent of it was unrecognizable. The big bathroom was replaced with a nurse's station and there were many single rooms for bedrooms. As I looked up at Ed, I gestured to him to venture forward down the corridor. It was so different then forty-five years ago, with modern decorations and furnished with large screen televisions and little kitchenettes with all up to date appliances. This was "freedom" to the utmost, but it was still an institution, where patients were told what to do and when.

While Ed wheeled me out of the unit, I looked up at him and said "Those demons ran down the mountain quickly! Now they are free, too. Maybe they will take up skiing in late November!" As usual, he just directed his glance at me saying "Only you would say such a thing, Gail!" Once on the outside of the wood trimmed glass door, I just needed a picture so I could look back knowing my ghosts were freed. Free at last, free at last!

Knowing that Ed had enough of this journey down memory road, I persuaded him to let me see the new additions such as the gym, library and pool. Nice, but once again the place still had that look and feel of an institution as we went up and down in the elevator, which looked like the original, leading to long, never ending, cold corridors leading to who knows where.

Soon I was at the entrance which led to the "real" world, realizing I never had to wheel through those doors ever again if I chose not to. I did my time here approximately forty-five years ago for a period of fourteen months in all and now I could hold my head up and smell the fresh air of FREEDOM.

CHAPTER FOUR

MY DREAMS AND NIGHTMARES

After Crotched Mountain Rehab Center, my schooling experiences were even more appalling. I had some home schooling for six months with a teacher who was my brother's forth grade teacher at some point. Miss Walsh was strict and an old maid who really pushed me to the limit. I guess she knew how capable I was and looking back, this was a positive thing for me, because someone had faith in me.

Searching through my school records I'm finding out that my parents tried to enroll me into the Massachusetts Hospital School in Canton. There were the usual humdrum psychological and physical examinations with the same conclusions. "Your daughter has extreme Cerebral Palsy who needs twenty-four around the clock hospital care, etc., etc."

"Her communication skills are extremely impaired."

The major thing that brought all this to an end was the provision that I wasn't to be allowed to go home on any weekends, but only on certain holidays such as Thanksgiving, Christmas and Easter. There wasn't any way I could do this because I was so attached to my family!

In 1973 , the saga continued when I again applied to the school, but now rejection was due to my age, grade level and the shortage of state and federal funds.

The Commonwealth of Massachusetts

Department of Public Health

Donald C. Gates, M.D.
Superintendent
ADDRESS ALL COMMUNICATIONS TO THE
SUPERINTENDENT

Massachusetts Hospital School

Canton, Massachusetts 02021

June 20, 1973

Mrs. San Filippo
257 Vine Street
Everett, MA 02149

Dear Mrs. San Filippo:

The Committee on Admissions has carefully considered your application for Gail as a Day Student at the Hospital School and feels it is not practical or realistic to attempt a school admission for 10 months. The law under which the Hospital School operates requires the discharge of any patient/student at twenty-one (21) years of age.

Although she has good intelligence the facilities and programs of the Hospital School do not lend themselves to meet her needs. Having last attended approximately the 8th grade, at the age of twenty (20) she would not readily fit in amongst the younger children. Unfortunately, we have no special classes or special tutors to meet the special individual needs which she requires.

During the past year we have been short two regular teachers and next year without Federal Funds we will be without teacher-aides, who have been so helpful in the past in assisting those unable to use their hands or with marked speech impairments.

Under ideal conditions of education we would make every effort to increase her studies in such ways as we could. If indeed circumstances change and appropriate additions to the School staff are possible such as to provide entire care and assistance in her studies, I will be in touch with you.

With kind wishes.

Sincerely yours,

Donald C. Gates, M. D.
Superintendent

DCG:k

43

Then at about age eleven I attended Kennedy Hospital Day School in Brighton, Massachusetts for about four years. Each day I got driven there in a taxi cab. This was an experience within itself. I had several drivers, but mainly three men.

One was this old man who could only speak Italian and swore persistently over everything. Along with this, he was incessantly spitting out of his window. He was the most disgusting and repulsive human being I ever met at that point in my life.

Another driver was Howard Jackson. Howard was kind to me, but he had this habit of talking about his alcoholism problem. I wished he did not do this while I was being driven by him because it made me a little uneasy.

At the age of fourteen, I had this taxi cab driver named Mac. Mac was my favorite cab driver. He treated me with respect and kindness. Although he looked much older because of his wrinkled and ruddy complexion, he was only fifty-seven years old which I thought was ancient. Now at age of fifty-three, I know better. Mac was the candy man in these days, giving me a Mounds candy bar each time he drove me from school. I heard much later that when other drivers refused the order to drive me, Mac always was there for me and became a very special individual in my life.

The second year at Kennedy, I recall that I had an excellent teacher named Miss Kane, who clearly showed how much she loved her job just by her enthusiasm. Each day we had a schedule, which was unlike the other teachers there. That year I swear I learned more than in the three other years combined.

The remaining three years we had teachers who just did not give a damn about their job, but looking back I realize the reasons for this. Imagine having a classroom with students of different handicaps and learning problems? In another year we had an old hag named Mrs. McGinty for a teacher, complete with her white hair and big butt. She turned out to be a complete bitch by making fun of a few other students for their inabilities to do math. She should have had been reported at the time, but at fifteen one was afraid of the repercussions.

Yes, schooling at Kennedy was not very good because they placed all the students together without thinking about their ability to learn. Plus, we had the nuns to keep us in line. I recall that in confessions I used to make up sins that I never even committed or even understood. One of the made up confessions was in answer to the questions about whether I thought of evil ideas or lying. Of course, I denied these acts by confessing a straight up "No."

While other students were doing second grade math, I was doing fifth grade. The whole system was wrong as so many so-called Special Classes in Massachusetts were at that time. We were all mixed and put together.

It was during this time I met a new friend, Alice. Although she was a few months older than me, we got along fine. She also had Cerebral Palsy, but she was able to do a lot more than me physically. Although she was in a wheelchair, I believed she could have walked around with crutches if she had chosen. One day she told me how she got Cerebral Palsy and it had quite an impact on me at the time. A high fever at two years old did it, while the doctor sat back at home giving instructions to her parents to give her cool baths and a couple of baby aspirins. After the fever had gone down, it was discovered that it had damaged part of her brain. She told me she had to start all over again, learning how to crawl, etc.

From 1964 until about three years ago we were the best of friends, going through our own turmoil and disappointments. In later years, the friendship ended due to a variety of reasons involving jealousy and envy.

It was at Kennedy that I received my Confirmation at about age fourteen, two years after I started. This was a very special event in my life because Cardinal Cushing, a very well known cardinal in the 1960's , performed the ceremony. He was as I pictured him: a tall and gentle spoken man.

It was during this time that I got drawn into the Cerebral Palsy Group of Greater Boston, which was started by Edith Schneider, a woman with Cerebral Palsy herself, back in the sixties. The group's philosophy is that no matter what kind of handicap one may have, an individual could overcome and cope with limitations if he or she tried. Mrs. Schneider was a great, educated, and inspirational woman not only for us with Cerebral Palsy, but to all our hundreds of volunteers with whom we have traveled throughout the four decades. She married a lawyer, Sydney Schneider, and they had a daughter, Rachael, who used to frequently go with us on various occasions and trips. I wondered through the years if she ever resented her parents being disabled and introducing or pushing her into our world. I know now that no matter how a child grows up, he/she has problems of some kind . They could be rich or poor, black or white, etc., and most have their own psychological issues brewing in their souls.

After I got out of Kennedy Day School in 1968 I once again had home schooling for about a year by Miss Walsh. I can still see her to this day, approximately thirty-five or so years later, as a typical spinster, with her graying hair always tied back as she sat beside me instructing me in the principles of math and spelling. It was here that I decided not to become a math scholar. I simply thought that math was the most dull and pointless subject, except addition and subtraction. What in the hell was I going to do with this knowledge? I sure was not going into banking or accounting, so what was the sense? For weeks I really didn't like Miss Walsh but looking back she was a very good teacher and I learned a lot from her. But I was getting antsy again and needed to get out of the house as I was sick of looking at the same four walls, with for the most part only my mother around to communicate with.

This was when I had heard of a local school for boys and girls my age that have disabilities also, so I decided I would go there, mostly just to get out of the house. The name of the place was Hogan Regional Center located about ten miles north of Everett, where we lived. I had no idea of the kind of school it really was until I started my first week or two. I soon discovered its purpose. It was basically a place for the parents to put not only their physically impaired kids, but ones who were severely mentally retarded too. I was horrified over what I had to see the nurse's aids, instructors and so-called teachers do to these helpless individuals day after day, five days a week. Especially during lunchtime, when I was wheeled to the cafeteria, I had to see young individuals sitting on the floor drumming their heads against the walls. It was like they knew the chaos which was going on inside that place. It was the chaos of the mind which ninety-nine percent of us try to avoid or ignore every day and every moment, but the difference between us and them was they could not escape their demons due to a mental illness or a form of mental retardation such as autism. They were locked up behind bars which could not be seen. Many years later, I found out that a former Personal Care Attendant of mine, Lynne, who I happened to meet online, had worked at Hogan in the early nineties and I learned how badly she had treated these poor, innocent victims if they did not do as she said . I only listened then, just saying to myself this would never be me. But about nine years later, I was drawn into her power and forced to have a onetime homosexual experience with her. While the next long months dragged by, she began playing other head trips on me by telling me how many hours she was going to be working, etc. This happening, and another in particular, were the worst things I need to confess and come to terms within myself for the rest of my days on this earth. I cheated on my soul mate and not thinking of what effect it would have on him and others. Control was and is the biggest aspect of life so I will not make any excuses for myself. I had choice. The clients in Hogan didn't. In almost every aspect of life, there is something outside of our own free will that tries to control us. It forces us to travel into our minds and reevaluate our notion of freedom and how many choices are really are own.

At Hogan, instead of treating the students with dignity and respect the staff would jump on top of them and hold them down if they started acting out due to their pent up frustration at being unable to express themselves due to autism or a similar mental disability. Or they would just allow individuals to hit their heads on the cafeteria or classroom walls repeatedly. Looking back now it seems to me that it was a control issue. An example of this for me was when I signed up for a workshop on making greeting cards for the gift shop. The instructor, Sheila, simply said we would be getting paid twenty-five weekly. Of course, I thought she meant twenty-five dollars a week. When she handed me a quarter at the end of the week, I was appalled. If I had the use of my hands I would have slapped her and said to her fat face "You know where you can put that quarter!" but I took her abuse like a two year old as she wheeled me into a corner because I was refusing her demands. During these couple of minutes of humiliation, I asked my girlfriend, Alice, (from Kennedy) to wheel me out of the room and to get help for me. The teacher, Rob Vincent, who worked full-time and was a genuinely caring man toward his students, came running to help me. It was people like me who made Rob's job worth while. He was the person I went to when the world came crashing down on me. He was a kind, patient and hippie type of guy with his long, flowing black hair tied back. Rob Vincent was one of my heroes, and he remains to this very day wherever he may be. The last time I saw Rob was eleven years ago this past September when he just came over to my apartment on the Lynnway in Lynn, Massachusetts to have lunch at the Porthole Restaurant and to talk, laugh and cry over events we had been through in 1971 through 1973 when we last saw each other. This is a friend to me. He, with many others, such as Mrs. Kent, Beverly Wilson (the music instructor who got me hooked on Carole King) and, of course, Joel Larson, who left Hogan in June of 1972 to supposedly go back to school for a degree in psychology. He returned to work at Hogan a decade later which I never understood because the clients need to be prescribed medications and only doctors can do this. Prior to his departure he aided me in my escape and advancement out of Hogan Regional Center as soon as he could by writing letter after letter to colleges and the Massachusetts Hospital School in Canton. They actually wanted me to go directly to Gordon College but I told them I was not prepared since I was just then studying to take the GED Exam. I had so little schooling that I knew I needed a high school education of some sort.

I often had individual help from certain teachers and instructors while I was at Hogan. One of them was an art instructor, Mrs. Ruth O'Keefe, a really kind middle aged woman and a volunteer at Hogan for a year or so. Mrs. O'Keefe was keen to my love of art and therefore spent a good amount of time teaching me different techniques to enhance my paintings. She seemed very impressed at how I used my head stick to paint the picture I was working on, which I shall get into in more detail later.

It was during the third week of September of 1973 when I was twenty that I got finally accepted into the Massachusetts Hospital School, but not before my mother and father took me in to meet the principal, Miss Lorraine Atkins. I got accepted into the school after many letters of recommendation from instructors and even from senators. Miss Atkins, who was an exceedingly, professional woman, just said "I have never in my work here received so many letters on a student."

I got into the Massachusetts Hospital School with a lot of determination and fighting the system due to my age. I was accepted with a couple of regulations. First, I had to be on the Honor Roll every semester with only A's and B's . Second, my mother had to volunteer a certain number of hours a week to help other students to write papers or take tests. Mrs. Brown and Mrs. Copely were the other teacher's aids and they were as different in temperament as day and night. I still can hear Mrs. Brown's soft, serious voice whispering in the library while Mrs. Copely's tone of voice and laughter echoed through the corridors like an adolescent girl.

I met Joel Larson again a few years ago and it did not turn out to be a pleasant experience. Even though he had helped me get into Massachusetts Hospital School, it turned out to be a very stressful experience in several ways for me. He pressured me into going in the Amway business by making numerous visits to my home. However, whenever I asked him how much it would cost to start, he never really answered my question. At this point, I knew he was baiting me and trying to reel me in. It did not take a genius to come to this conclusion. In the end, I did not take his bait.

At the present, I am trying to get my painting back that I stupidly gave him as a gift thirty odd years ago to put into this book, but much to my dismay he keeps on giving me excuses as to where the painting is . This picture took me two and a half months to paint with a head stick and with the help of my art instructor Ruth O'Keefe. I know that it is gone forever but some resolution came when I went to his office at Hogan on Tuesday, March 29, 2006 to tell him off.

As I entered the building that I had once crossed the threshold of so many years ago, I saw more than I wanted to remember. Everything was so stark, with cement floors down every corridor. I could hear the click of the nurses' high heels as they walked behind me, like ghosts of my past.

I showed my Personal Care Attendant, Joy, where the classroom was where I had sat during so many days of my teenage years. She was dismayed by the whole setup of the building and agreed with me that THIS WAS HELL! When I was there, although it was some thirty odd years ago, it had been a lot better. Back then it was not as institutionalized as it is today. I had a lot of laughs back then and a lot of fond memories to take with me.

When we asked where Mr. Larson's office was, we were brought down to the basement. I looked up at my attendant in horror. Where the hell were we going? We were in the bowels of the building. When I finally saw where he worked I was shocked. Here was a man who apparently had gone back to get his degree in psychology and he was sharing a hole in the wall with three other people. There was no ventilation and coffee was spilled over one of the desks. The walls were peeling and dirty, with old wrinkled memos taped to them. On his desk, a half eaten bowl of chowder was sitting in front of an empty chair.

When he finally walked in the door, his mouth almost hit the floor. He had to feign calmness and composure since one of his colleagues had returned and was sitting at his own desk. As he sat down in his chair, I became conscious of how appalling he looked with his large stomach hanging over his pants and the tell-tale ruddy complexion of an alcoholic. He looked simply terrible.

As the confrontation continued, it gave me the satisfaction I needed for my own peace of mind and closure. I will never forget how he was trying to avoid my words, but he could not. My words were loud and clear, and he understood everything. I had him cornered, literally, as he slumped in his chair trying to make phony small talk to mask the real issue. He knew why I was there and after the first smug question as to my welfare, I started to jump down his throat. I was not going to have any time wasted, because I knew that this would be my last opportunity to tell him what an asshole he was in regards to my painting. So I bluntly told him that he was a fucking asshole about four times over.

As he looked at me in shock, I do not think he believed I had it in me and he feigned ignorance and pretended he did not understand me. My loyal attendant, Joy spoke up and said calmly "Gail is saying that you are a fucking asshole! You are not the same person you were before." He replied that he was the same person and again tried to hoodwink me into believing he had the picture, he just had to look for it, and at which point I told him to forget it." You can take the picture and shove it up your ass!" I said to him. He looked at Joy again and she again told him what I had said. It was actually a very worthwhile experience for me because I was able to call him out for what he was, a fucking asshole. The man that had been sitting at the other desk heard all this and left the room once he realized Joel was in a tight spot. As I was wheeled out of the office I wished him the best sarcastically. I had closure and knew I would never have to see that institution again.

In the meantime, I found a photograph of my watercolor in one of my photo albums and enlarged it. It looks pretty good so I am thinking of bringing it to a professional camera store to see if they could make the picture even bigger.

The next three years after I made my big escape from Hogan Regional Center I attended Brayton High School at Massachusetts Hospital School in Canton. I found it to be gruel-ing. At one period I was taking two grades at once (11th and 12th) just to graduate sooner. It was altogether very different than what I was used to. There were days when I thought I was never going to make it, but I had to succeed and stick by their ludicrous regulations which only applied to me because of my age. This was opposite for students who were under nineteen years old who were sneaking in the bathrooms or going in back of the high school building to smoke weed. I was separated out in many ways because this was a test for me and if I failed it would only be my fault. The pressure to keep up my grades and persona were overwhelming at times. Sometimes I felt like I was on death row awaiting prosecution if I stepped out of line in any way. I was a puppet and if only a single string broke my life would go downhill. The only time I felt freedom was when I went driving my motorized chair all over campus. The wheelchair weighed over two hundred pounds without me in it and to this very day I can't imagine my Dad ever bringing it down our backstairs with me in it to the bus or my van . Plus, neither had a ramp or lift. Now I know how I contributed to his bad health and stress.

The teacher who taught freshman, sophomore, junior and senior English classes was Mr. Robert Haiduke who was an odd sort of a man with his own slant on life. I recall he was spiritual in his own way but in a weird twist, he used to believe in tarot cards, which I thought was strange. I guess nobody truly respected or liked him because he was like a Dr. Jekyll and Mr. Hyde kind of person where every day he would act differently. One day he could be as sweet as pie but on the next day Mr. Haiduke could be his own worst enemy. As the years passed by, I saw and noticed how he bullied many of the other students and I just sat there not having the guts to talk back to him, until one day I just could not listen to his abuse any more. I call it the day of "The Surprise Quiz." As all of my classmates looked at each other in surrender, I spoke out to this man for the first time in my life. I told him I was not taking any test and just turned on my motorized wheelchair and began maneuvering toward the principal's office. Before I reached the classroom doorway, he asked me to stop because he knew I meant business. He actually apologized to me in front of the entire class. From that day, he gave the respect that he owed to all students .

Then there was Mr. Gibbs who was the most sincere and placid gentleman that I ever met in my life. He always was well dressed five days a week in a suit jacket and tie , without a single ashen piece of hair out of place. He taught math and typing. I never knew how he got mixed up teaching typing for students who were taking the business course. I only knew if I was older, he would be my ideal man.

Science was taught by Mrs. Claire Pickett in my freshman year. Oh my God, I do not know how I ever remembered all of those chemistry symbols in my freshman year. And, then came algebra and geometry, which did not make a bit of sense to me at all. I vividly recollect asking Mrs. Pickett "Where am I ever going to use this information in my life time?" She just answered "It will develop your mind." Sure? But I do need to say Mrs. Pickett was a saint and a great teacher.

Mr. John Sinnot was a very attractive man with his blond hair parted on one side, but very, very shy. His face used to turn beet red whenever one of us said anything at all out of his comfort zone and this was so easy to do. One example was when some female students made comments or gestures toward other male students. He taught one of my favorite subjects, Civics or social studies. Just remembering dates of wars boggled my mind.

Science class was with Mr. Andy Hildreth. He actually looked like a scientist with his bald head and spectacles. I was never much for biology so it just blew me away the day when we had to dissect a small frog or some small creature. No matter what it was, I surely skipped class that day!

Then, of course, there was a physical therapist just for the day students. Her name was Wanda. Wanda was tough, but she was your typical physical therapist who wanted us to do exercises for the hell of it. This was just her job in life, to aggravate us! It's proof of the small world we live in when Wanda would enter my life again nineteen years later when I met Ed. Wanda happens to be Ed's aunt.

In March of 1975 my schooling had to become second priority in my life because I had to have major back surgery or else my lungs would collapse over time. I had scoliosis which is a curvature of the spine. I had suffered from it for years and finally my parents knew I would now definitely need the operation to correct it. Then the search for the right doctor began. I do not know how my mom found out about Dr. John Hall being the best in the field, but prior to my seeing him I sat in several orthopedic clinics over a two year period hearing different physicians' opinions on how to treat me. In time, my parents realized I was the guinea pig once more when doctors suggested performing many procedures prior to my back operation. They wanted me in body casts on every part of my body. Sure they were going to take care of it, if they did not kill me first! Someone with scoliosis usually is operated on in one's early teens because bones usually are not fully developed by then. I went under the knife twice and had to stay in the hospital for six weeks. Both of my operations were done by Dr. John Hall, who was the best orthopedic surgeon from around the world. During the first operation, he took out one of my rib bones and placed it in my back. This operation was called the Dwyer procedure where screws and band devices are placed to correct spinal deformities. I had a body cast put on after this surgery. This cast went from under my armpits to my pelvis to keep me still. Other patients who had a similar operation were put in a metal apparatus called a Striker Frame Bed, which allowed no disturbance in the healing process. These patients would be turned on their backs and stomachs every few hours by the nurses. Seeing others unable to move made me think of a cross because when they were turned on their stomach their arms were secured to pieces of wood and their forehead rested on a thin strap of cloth to support it. In addition, spike like nails were secured into their temples to support their necks, kind of like being cooked on a rotisserie grill. I do not know which method was worse, swinging and being twirled around in the air every two hours or being confined, in my instance, to a body cast. At any rate, I began to develop this rash under my back cast which nobody could see or feel. One day I felt like my back was on fire. I told the nurse, but, of course, she did not listen. (I was only a cripple who did not know any better). The next day the cast was sawed off and my back was completely raw due to urine going up my back from the bed pan. The look of horror upon their faces gave me the satisfaction I deserved. After all, I knew what I was talking about! When my parents came up to visit me that afternoon, I was in a plastic tent. My mother, not understanding why I was in this tent ,became livid, saying to the nurses "My daughter knows when something is wrong! She's only physically disabled." Two weeks later , much to my dismay I went in for a second operation, which I had not expected. This one consisted of a Harrington rod and screws being placed in my back because the doctor wanted my back strong due to the excessive movement which sometimes goes along with having Cerebral Palsy. Dr. Hall was right in his judgment, but at that time I did not take the news very well. I was so disheartened when he told me this I started crying until I could not cry anymore. One of Dr. Hall's interns, Dr. Steven Stern, sat beside my bedside as I cried and cried. He really had a lot of compassion for me which I sure needed right then, because it seemed like no one else really comprehended what I was feeling inside. I had really believed I was going home and the news of a second operation came as a total shock to me. Due to a shortness of space, the floor that I had my room on also housed children and teenage cancer patients. I will never forget the wails of those children in pain and this was only one reason I did not want to have to stay in the hospital any longer. As I look back, this was hell. Thirty-one years later I still hear those children screaming in pain and torment. This will never go away.

The single escape from this nightmare was when the 11 P.M. to 7 A.M. shift came on duty. They had their hands full when they arrived on my unit. We were all wide awake from doing nothing all day. After all, we had slept half the day and night so by this time we were ready for some serious action. We could not get out of our beds to let off steam during the day. At about midnight the television came to life. Myself and the three other gals I was sharing the room with needed a double dose of stimulation and we were hell bent on getting it. Shortly after the television started blaring, the click, click, click of the nurses shoes started rumbling through the hallway like distant thunder. We looked at each other with half bent smiles awaiting their arrival. It was tremendously funny and we got a lot of belly laughs because we already knew what the nurses were going to say.

Although they knew it was a waste of breath they sighed and ran through the rules with us again, like a broken record. They never got anywhere so they actually started to laugh too because they knew damn well what our situation was and so let us get away with it. After all they knew there was nothing they could do. We all said "How can we be sleepy if all we do is lie in our beds all day?" Some nights we had parties to mask the boredom. I can only imagine what Dr. Hall would say if he ever came unexpectedly!

After six weeks I was released from the hospital and went home to do another six months of bed rest. My parents purchased a stretcher for me just so I would not have to look at the four walls of my bedroom. They would slide me onto the stretcher to the station wagon and take me for rides so I could enjoy the fresh outside air. My recuperation period was a difficult time for me. I was bored out of my mind but the biggest downfall came when my parents told me the high school I had been attending had sent my parents a notice that they would not be accepting me back. I don't know what my parents said to the powers that were at the school but I went back in September 1975 for my senior year. It was another fight, but another victory. My Dad and Mother used to drive me to school five days a week and, at times, my Dad slept in the car while I attended classes. (I heard my English teacher reporting "Some bum is down in the garage sleeping in a beige Chevy station wagon!" I guess Miss Atkins laughed and told him "He's Gail's father. He works nights and drives Gail here everyday." I graduated with Honors and was selected to write the alumni speech. I remember relatives, family and friends came to celebrate one of the biggest day and accomplishments of my life.

As a graduation gift, my parents gave me a certificate to the Medieval Manor Restaurant in Boston for four people.

Chapter Five

My College Life

If or where I was going to college was literally all up to me. The guidance counselor I had in high school, himself handicapped with Polio, was discouraging when I told him that I wanted a college education. This Mr. Samuels was against any discussion about going on to college so I realized I had to do it alone. So, I did. I applied to Massachusetts Bay Community College and University of Massachusetts in Boston. I got accepted into both but chose University of Massachusetts because it was a four year program.

Right after the summer of 1976 I enrolled at the University of Massachusetts campus in Boston as a part time student.

For awhile I had The Ride , a public bus service for seniors and disabled people, drive me to school. I mostly had a main driver named Bob Hagen for about a year or so. He had blond hair and a smile that would knock your socks off. I became quite good friends with Bob , his brother , and his girlfriend Beth.

On my invitation, Bob even went away to Nassau back in 1979 with the CP Group. He was a good volunteer but, as the week went on, I can say I got to know the other part of him. I knew that he smoked marijuana but he also had a few more bad habits. Anyway, I begged him prior to going to the airport to throw away or get rid of whatever else he had on him. Due to my stupidity and ignorance twenty-six and a half years ago, I believed his story that he flushed whatever he had down the toilet. However, I learned differently when we got on the plane and I discovered that he still had the dope on him. I guess then I knew what type of person he was and probably would remain the rest of his life.

Years later, either my Mom and Dad or Mom and Auntie Muriel (who at the time worked for me as a Personal Care Attendant for a year or two before and after college) drove me back and forth to college. I learned a valuable lesson from this move as well. This was the knowledge never to hire family.

There is always that disappointment or disagreement which follows that cannot on any account possibility be forgotten. One of the biggest issues was when my aunt found out she wasn't getting paid on our numerous shopping sprees and remedied this by saying she had to get home for my cousin with Down's syndrome or to prepare my Uncle Jackie's supper! In the meantime, my mom took on the task of caring for my nephew Danny, my sister's first child, while my sister went back to work as a medical secretary at the Deaconess Hospital in Boston four days a week. To this day, I really do not know how my Mom ever had time or the stamina to do everything she did. As my sister dropped off my three month old nephew Danny at 7:15 four days a week, my Mom was in the process of getting me up and dressed. While this was all happening my Dad was coming in from his graveyard shift, singing, joking around and preparing breakfast. Of course, my Dad was wide awake and full of vim and vigor. He was even like this when all three of us(my brother, sister and I) were going to grade school. He'd come into our bedrooms singing "Good morning, breakfast clubbers, how do you do?" How my sister hated mornings anyway and this irritated her more. I can still hear in the back of my mind how she used to say "Dad, no more!" Thinking about it now, it was annoying!

College was a whole new experience in that I was competing with the able bodied population as I had never actually done before. In a sense, I was in the real world for the first time in my life. I was free and I realized I had free will of my own. If I wanted to go to a class, I did. Otherwise, I rode off in my chin operated, motorized wheelchair to wherever I wanted to go. My favorite place on campus was in back of Building 2 . I went there just to have some time alone while overlooking the water toward Castle Island . I could also see Carson Beach and Pleasure Bay. This whole area is a twenty-two acre urban park along the South Boston shoreline of Dorchester Bay. As I sat there looking at the pleasure boats going by, my mind traveled elsewhere. I thought about past happenings in my life and wondered what if I had played the games differently. Would my life be better? It was during these forty-five minute intervals that I wondered about my whole life ahead of me.

College was extremely difficult with having to tape record each class and transcribe it down on paper when I got home. Unlike other students, I was not physically able to use my hands to write down notes, but nevertheless I recorded all my classes and jotted down the important information for exams or papers. This single task of putting down notes from a tape recorder took me hours of pressing the play, stop and rewind buttons of my tape recorder with my head stick even though I only took two or three classes each semester. When it came time for term papers, I first found the information I needed to prove my theory, folded the pages and placed the books open all over my bed. My Mom did not have the slightest idea what I was doing. All she said to me was "I can't believe how you are doing this, Gail" . Looking back now, over twenty plus years later, I myself do not know how I ever did it. Being a part time student, I either had my classes on Tuesdays and Thursdays or Mondays, Wednesdays and Fridays so I could have time to do homework. This was the first big challenge in my life. All in all, we had a refuge at college where we could spout out or just relax. The Disabled Center was our very own to just talk or to vent. The center was headed by Andrea Shein and other able bodied students who worked with us . We were able to hide or make our escape without judgment or ridicule. Andrea was a type of person whom I never met prior to my going to the University of Massachusetts. It was like she was disabled in a past life and understood the issues and prejudices we had to confront. Andrea was always there for me when professors and society ridiculed me for being in their classes or presence.

I usually had understanding professors, but there was always that single instructor with that look of doubt and apprehension on his/her face as each semester began. Also, my fellow classmates did not know what to make of me. I drove my motorized chair all over campus , which consisted of four buildings: administration/library/bookstore, the science building, the English/Psychology/Sociology building and the gym. In between classes the halls were so crowded either with students standing around or dilly dallying, I had to place my wheelchair speed on high to just make them move. They had only two choices, to move or get run over by a wheelchair that weighed approximately two hundred pounds or more.

The only huge obstacle with being in a wheelchair was when it snowed or rained. I solved this by going down to the garage in the nearest elevator and traveling through the underground tunnels to the other buildings. Looking back now I would never in my wildest dreams ever do this nowadays with such lunatics in this world! I could have had been raped or killed.

My major was English for three years. I enjoyed the major except for the everlasting reading of writers such as Shakespeare and Edgar Allen Poe , who I thought must have been taking drugs when they wrote. I took these courses with numerous instructors, like Professor Louise Smith with her long, flowing, light, highlighted hair and Professor Katz ,who had this soft voice which he projected throughout each class. When I heard months later that he had once worked in a correctional institution it blew my persona of him. He was such a nice gentleman in the classroom. Who would ever dream he worked with the slime of this earth ? Little did he know that I had cheated on one exam that he allowed me to take home! Although it was an open book test, he expected us students to recall where we had read lines and quotes from this hundred or so page literature book. My main reason for taking English as a major in the first place was largely due to my career intentions and interest in writing. I always dreamed of writing professionally. My dreams came to an end when I took a course in drama and received a D! This was the first D that I ever received in my life.

As the years rolled along, I changed my major from English to Sociology and took many law and justice courses . I met many more interesting professors. Professor Movahedi was a Sociology instructor who taught several courses such as Social Psychology, Social Psychiatry and Statistics. He was one of my favorite professors. The first time I met him he seemed to be a very shy man with a receding hairline and black rimmed glasses. When he began his first lecture I could not understand a word he was saying due to his thick Iranian accent. Maybe it was just me but as I took a quick look around the classroom I think I saw the same look of apprehension on other students' faces. I questioned myself about whether I should stay or go and , if I left, how I would retrieve my tape recorder ,which was right in front of him , without causing a scene. As the forty-five minutes went by I saw this teacher for what he really was. Unlike many others I had, this teacher had his own distinct sense of humor and a smile and laugh that were extremely contagious. I saw that familiar look of doubt in his eyes in the first week or so but he turned out to understand my speech much better than other professors. Maybe it was that, in a sense, we both had distinct accents of our own. I took about four classes with him. I remember this one class in particular when he was talking about the Holocaust and how each one of us could perform similar actions and behaviors against the Jewish population. All of us in the class disagreed with him, indicating "What an awful thing to say." Then Professor Movahedi talked about an experiment done by Stanley Milgram, a social psychologist who in 1979 wrote a paper called "The Obedience Experiment: Authority, Legitimacy, and, Human

Action." Milgram learned that if under a strong force of authority people willingly administered painful shocks to an innocent victim strapped to an electric chair. Milgram's reasoning for this behavior was that most people do not have the internal resources to resist authority and will proceed to administer serious harm to others when in a formal authoritarian setting. I wonder what that says about peoples' treatment of the disabled.

Aside from Sociology, Professor Movahedi was a great help when I had to grudgingly take Statistics as a requirement. I swear I went up to his office at least once a week to have him explain a simple equation to me. I just did not get it or did not want to understand the concepts. I never had that math ability for some reason.

It was during these years that I got involved in the unfairness of the life for disabled citizens. The barrier and inaccessibility issues came up when a group of us found out we could not go to any Friday's restaurants due to the different levels they had in every restaurant they constructed. One day a huge group of us picketed right in front of a Friday's in Boston. They were outraged because not only were we disturbing their business but we had called one of the news stations to capture our actions.

Another incident came years later when a huge number of us from all over Massachusetts in fact took over the Boston State House to protest the low pay for our Personal Care Attendants. We were everywhere yelling, screaming and chanting. The governor, I think it was Wells at the time, disappeared out a back door we later learned. What a CHICKEN he turned out to be!

Several obstacles got in my way of my good experience at U. Mass, the two toughest ones being two Professors. One was an art teacher who told me outright that she did not want me to take her course. The class was in art appreciation so it did not encompass any drawing. Regardless of her apprehension, I took the course and my grade ended up to be a B. The other class was in music appreciation with Professor Cleveland. He was a big, lofty chap with a rude attitude towards me from the very beginning. He literally told me he did not want me in his classroom. Of course I stayed and received the highest mark in the class. I will always remember my dad and mom bringing my electric IBM typewriter up to Professor Cleveland's private office, setting me up with my head stick and seeing the look on his face. As he placed the final test in front of me I went to town in answering the questions. Every couple of minutes I felt him peeking over my shoulder and just uttering under his breath "Oh, my God." Since that day, he always went out of his way to say hello to me when I was wheeling to classes.

During the last two semesters of college I volunteered to work on Exceptional Parent Magazine as the chief international coordinator on the pen pal section. This required me to match up other parents, siblings, friends and professionals who had or knew a child or children with the same disability or birth disorders. It was particularly interesting but heartbreaking to read and go through these heart wrenching letters that came to me. Yes, I am disabled, but Cerebral Palsy is not inherited. Also, I had to dedicate a lot of time to this and in combination with my regular academic work, there were nights I was up until two o'clock in the morning matching people up. I did this in the hopes of getting this as a full time paying job after graduation, but it fell through due to the lack of funds.

About two years later I opened up a similar type of business from home with the aid of my sister and Massachusetts Rehabilitation counselor, John, but the business never got off the ground. It was on the same concept as "Exceptional Parent," but named "Friends, Inc."

When I graduated on May 22 1983, I call to mind it was a beautiful, sunny and breezy day. As I drove with my Dad, Mom, Sister Nancy and my nine month old nephew Danny towards Boston, I could feel my stomach going into knots. The thought of being in front of three hundred people, including uncles, aunts, cousins, Nana Campbell and friends, in my motorized chair scared the shit out of me. What if I took a spasm and drove my chair right off the platform. Andrea, who was the coordinator of the Disabled Center, asked earlier if I wanted someone to wheel me in the ceremony, but I said " NO WAY. I have made it this far, so I can do anything!" All I can remember is being dropped off at the Disabled Office to put on my black, loose fitted robe and cap with yellow tassels dangling from it and feeling like I was going in front of a firing squad. This was my moment of truth and proof of my willpower, receiving a piece of a paper which took seven years to earn and to own forever. As the hundreds of graduate's names were being called out in alphabetical order, I felt my heart pounding faster and faster. When they came to the letter "R" I got myself in a panic mode. What if I took a spasm and accidentally drove my chair right off of the platform in front of the hundreds of people in the audience? What a fool I would feel and look like! So, with this thought, I allowed my mind to think of the times I spent in back of Building 2 looking at the serene bay and missing some professor's boring, prolonged lecture. When my name was finally called I turned on my wheelchair and steered it with my chin control with no effort at all, as I heard in the background people clapping and cheering me on. The most ironic thing happened then. The professor who gave me a D gave me my diploma with a big smile on his face!

Afterwards, my parents had made reservations at a well known restaurant in Marblehead, Massachusetts named Rosalie's to celebrate with family and a few of my friends.

That September, I went back thinking about working towards my Masters but after taking one course I just decided against it. I was so sick of the whole 10 year journey I took, which included high school. I was just burned out.

Then in the fall of 1984 I took a few courses at Bunker Hill Community College in Charlestown, Massachusetts for Computer Programming where I studied Basic and Cobol programming. It was so damn boring that I got my behind out of there fast. It still sticks in my mind when all of the computers went down one afternoon and I had typed in three quarters of my program. All that hard work was gone in a ten seconds. Luckily, I had an understanding instructor who offered to copy my paper over into the computer. Everything had to be written to perfection or else the program was a bomb. Patience I have, but endurance I do not.

During my late teens and twenties, as you can see, I was mostly involved in getting an education so dating never came into the picture. Education was mostly my whole existence. It was in my early and mid teens when I felt otherwise because I was surrounded by my cousins and sister with their boyfriends, walking hand in hand or cuddled up side by side in each other arms. I guess I envied them at times. Who would go out or want to date me anyways? During these years I was focusing on getting a proper education which was denied me for so long that I didn't believe I needed other outside influences or distractions. And who in the world would be interested in dating me? Just the stigma of being in a wheelchair was a turn off to most guys. Maybe it would come one day, but if it didn't, it didn't.

Chapter Six

My Father

My Dad was the most loving and mentally supportive father I could have asked for . He died suddenly on June 7, 1988 from a heart attack after suffering two previous ones during the early 1980s. It was the most devastating heartache I have ever felt or expect to feel again in my entire life. I did not want to live anymore for a time during my long mourning period.

That Tuesday morning he did not look at all well. The color in his face was grayish, just like death. My sister and I were out in the back yard with my small nephew and niece, sunning ourselves, while my parents came out to say they were going out to do some errands and the visit the dentist. As soon as we laid eyes on my Dad out in the daylight we knew something was wrong. He promised us he would go to the hospital just up the street but afterwards we were told that he went to Health Stop instead. I guess they took his vital signs and released him to die an hour a half later. In retrospect, we probably should have sued them for their negligence. One minute he was preparing a supper of chicken cutlets and fifteen minutes later my Mom checked on him in bed and started screaming. He had stopped breathing. Then it was complete bedlam. While my Mom was in utter confusion, I sat in my wheelchair yelling for anyone to come and help. Finally a neighbor, who lived next door, and my sister, who at that time lived on the next street adjacent to us in a four family duplex which my Dad and Mom owned, came in and tried to understand me. I was a mess. My sister tried to give my Dad CPR as we waited in vain for the ambulance but time elapsed into minutes without any professional medical help and I think we all knew that it was too late. We really realized this when the ambulances and police finally arrived and did nothing. I never saw my father carried out of the house because I was in the kitchen, but I knew. We all knew, except my Mom.

Now as I look back at those next five days it seemed like a dream that I hoped I would wake up from. But this was not a dream as the house filled up with family, relatives and friends. As each came through our door to pay their respects, each person had a look of disbelieve all over his/her face. This could not be happening. I think at the wake it all became reality as I saw my Dad laying in the beautiful coffin, thinking to myself how often he had denied himself of so many luxuries while he was alive. While I screamed and cursed God, I also realized this was my father's fault. He knew for years he had a heart condition but he did not take care of himself with a better diet, exercise and self-respect. The rest of his wake, which seemed to last for weeks, I just numbed myself by drinking or taking valium before each wake. I did not want to feel anything. I was a robot performing my duty as a daughter. I just wanted to be numb until after the funeral. And I was until I was at the grave site, where I felt I left my body and was looking over the whole scene. Cars were never ending and family and friends were weeping and howling very loudly. My Grandmother Sanfilippo and my Mom had to be held up.

Suddenly, as the priest started his eulogy, I realized I was part of this terrible happening. My Dad was really gone forever and nothing would change this reality. As I wailed in a frenzy, I felt a hand on my shoulder. When I saw who it was it gave me strength. It was Ben, whom I had known for years as a Personal Care Attendant and volunteer at Cape Cod Cerebral Palsy. Ben was a very good friend, until he made moves on my sister in the summer of 1989.

After the funeral our house was full once more with people helping us through the start of the mourning stage. When they left hours later to resume their own lives, we were once again alone with our loss.

That summer my mom, sister, nephew, niece and myself went into seclusion at my parents' cottage in South Yarmouth to escape the ghosts on Vine Street. But to my dismay, my father's spirit was there, too. He loved it down at the cottage where there was a lot of laughter and good times since he had purchased it in 1972. Each summer, we had a new adventure.

I remember even to this day the frantic ordeal it was just getting packed to go down the Cape as my parents hauled the three of us to our cottage in South Yarmouth. These excursions began with the image of my Dad sitting in his orange bucket chair positioned in between the stove and refrigerator while my Mother hurried her way around the apartment to pack not only for the three of her children but for my Dad too. As the half hours ticked by, I could see my Dad getting more agitated as my Mom danced her way through each room in search for clothes, toiletries, toys and games for us as my father just sat put in that forsaken orange bucket chair twiddling his thumbs. Then the next move was to attempt to get everything into the car being sure there was room for three children and wife. Thinking back , I never did know how everything fit in the car, including my wheelchair.

Then came the big mind-numbing three hour car ride along roads twisting around the outer edges of the sea to Cape Cod along Route 3A. This drive I loathed immensely with the unremitting fighting and bantering which went on between my brother and sister and, of course, the question of "Are we there yet?" coming from my siblings' lips. Years down the line the trip to the Cape took on a new pattern when they made Route 3 which was a more direct highway, only taking us an hour and a half. The highlight of this drive was "Who will first spot the Sagamore Bridge?" which meant that we were three quarters of the way from the cottage. I came to believe my Dad benefitted from this game the most because there was complete stillness in the car for minutes while we focused our attention on the arising for the first sighting of the top of the bridge which could be barely seen between the branches of the hundreds of trees along Route 3. I later figured out why my Dad always sighted the bridge prior to us. He drove in the front seat and was the tallest! Crossing the suspension bridge gave me shivers because it only had two single lanes, one coming onto Cape Cod and the other coming off. If someone was not paying attention or drunk it would had been fatal disaster and it didn't help things when I saw a life-size billboard with the words "DESPERATE? SUICIDAL? PLEASE call the Samarians" at the number below if you feel suicidal "! I wondered just how many individuals actually did call when they got to this desperate point in their life and how many people in actual fact jumped? It was here when we knew there was another twenty or so miles to the cottage where we could run (or sit in my case), go to the beach or pond and just have fun.

With me in my chair, I realize now that the beach trips took some very hard work on the part of my parents. There were five of us to worry about. Either they dragged and pulled my wheelchair or my dad carried me through the uneven pillars of sand filled with shells bleached by the ocean to where the wheelchair awaited me. For the longest time we went to Sea Gull Beach which was right down the street from my Uncle Gordon's house. It was always crammed full so one day we drove down near the small canal where my father didn't have to pay. This area was picturesque and engaging for both the adults and us kids as the adults could oversee boats of all sizes coming up and down the path of the canal and take in the sights over on the opposite side of the inland waterway at Red Jacket Hotel while us kids dug for shells and steamers for that night's appetizer.

I particularly recall the time that we had a family of raccoons living in the fireplace. Not knowing this at the time, my sister built a fire and all of a sudden my Uncle Charlie (who was always joking) said "I hear something." Of course, we all just laughed and just said he was hearing things. A few minutes went by when my sister heard the soft cries of an animal. Sure enough, there was a whole family of raccoons living in our chimney , literally being cooked. The fire was put out fast and for the remainder of that night and into the early morning, we were coaxing raccoons out of our fireplace. My sister even caught one with gloves on. It was adorable but I myself do not love any animal from the rat family.

The other reminder of his was my Dad's favorite toy, his boat named "Edna May" which he purchased in the late 1960s. This thirty foot or so boat was his baby. It was docked in Saugus mostly, except when he brought it down the Cape where we all hold our own dear and frightening memories. One of the nice reminiscences was our boat ride over to an isolated island across from the Kennedy Compound. We used to drop anchor and relax and swim. We even saw some of the Kennedy clan such as Eunice Shriver who drove up on their own sail boats, basking in the sun. I still can call to mind how she looked with just a bra on and how old she appeared to be.

This boat gave some terrifying recollections, too. One day all the men (uncles, brother and dad) had this brilliant idea to go out fishing. Off they went but later, when the sun was drawing to a sunset, the men never came back through the cottage door. All the women paced the small house trying to look busy taking care of us kids but on their faces were looks of alarm and complete fright. All I recall was a deafening silence and tension in the air that could be cut with a knife. It was like they turned into robots trying so hard to hide every emotion in their bodies and minds. I believe it was around nine o'clock when the men came walking in like nothing was out of the ordinary. I later found out that men do not realize the concept of time.

A wonderful weekend was when my Dad invited all my uncles, aunts and cousins to our two bedroom cottage. I can still hear the talk and laughter on the patio that my Dad built himself and the smell of hamburgers, hot dogs, sausages, etc. By night fall there were so many activities going at once. The kitchen was where the women were playing Scrabble, Uno or Rummy while the boys watched some type of sports. There was the constant flow of coffee being dispensed to all. When 2:30 am came, I looked at my mother indicating to her with eye gestures enough is enough. I need to get out of my wheelchair, go pee and lay down somewhere. Anywhere. Everyone slept anywhere one could find room like on the couches, beds and even on the floor in between beds. I believe I slept out in the tent with my sister and ex brother-in-law in the front yard.

Yes, a lot of good times we had at my parents' cottage until my Dad's death.

Although it has been eighteen and a half years since my Dad's passing, sometimes time seems to have stood still. This very day I can still feel him around me like he never died.

I can still sense his presence around me protecting me from the world as he always had in my youth. I always think of a quote by Morrie in the book and movie "Tuesdays with Morrie" written by Mitch Albom, a former Sociology student of his, "Death ends a life, not a relationship."

The Sanfilippo Family

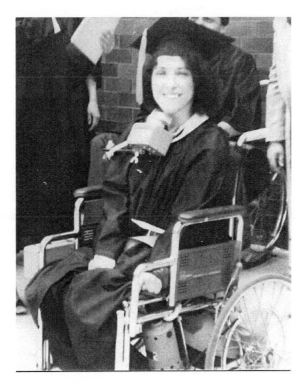

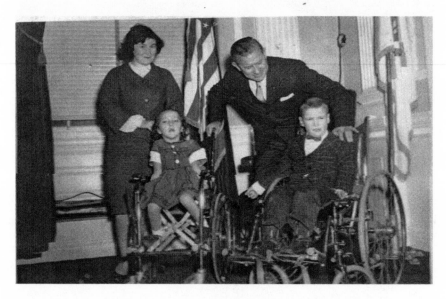

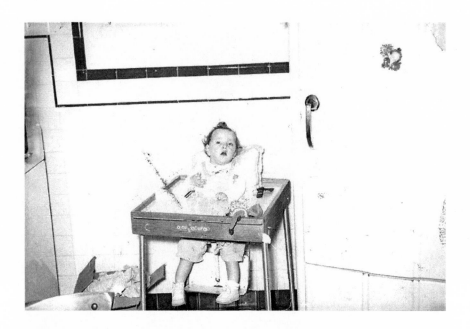

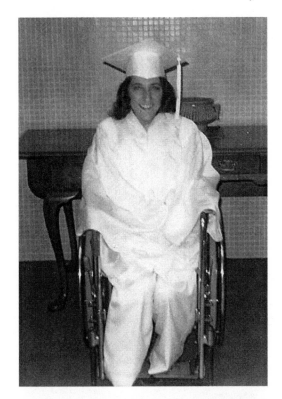

Chapter Seven

My Family Yesterday And Today

When I was older in my teens, my Uncle Jr. , who lived upstairs, used to come down-stairs some nights just to talk to my Mother at our kitchen table on his philosophy of life and religion. He was a twin of Rush Limbaugh, believing all that he said was right. He always had his own opinion and twist on a topic.

There was one night my Mother smoked her first marijuana joint with him. Of course, I am not supposed to know this, so hush, hush! But, let me tell you, my Mom and Uncle Junior thought they resolved a lot of the world's conflicts that night.

There is only one thing which I would like to obliterate from my mind. Uncle Junior sometimes came downstairs to sit and talk with my mother while my father was working on his usual graveyard shift from 11:00pm to 7:00am. On a couple of occasions, my mother and my uncle thought that my brother, my sister and I were fast asleep. The only problem was that I was not a good sleeper. I was actually a very light sleeper and the slightest noise in the house would wake me up. But this time it was coming from the downstairs hallway. It was odd to me because I was used to laying awake at night while my mother and Uncle Junior were talking to each other at the kitchen table, yet a couple of nights I was very aware that some kind of monkey business was going on in the hallway. I was old enough to know what certain sounds meant and the sounds from the hallway made my blood boil. If I had the ability to walk, I would have run down the hallway ready to kill. My heart is tortured even to this day. On occasion I used to ask my mother if she could explain to me what was going on but she always brushed me off and blamed it on an overactive imagination.

To this day, I look at my Mother with the conviction that she is losing a little of her memory somewhat because when we talk about other day by day happenings she does not recollect them. Then I say to myself maybe for survival she blocked certain recollections that are more agonizing than others . As the years go by I hope this choice of memories occurs to me.

In the writing of this book, I needed to know the real truth, so I emailed my uncle on January 11th -

---

Uncle Junior,

Love the stories you email me ALONG WITH 50 OTHER PEOPLE, but you NEVER ask me how I'm doing, E.T.C... Why is this? I grew up with you. You taught me SO FUCKING MUCH, ESPECIALLY how to talk and express myself, so give yourself some credit for this email I'm sending you, because if it wasn't for you I wouldn't be able to tell you to GO FUCK YOURSELF!!!!!!

I don't understand why you never ask me: How are you doing? How is Ed? Do you need anything? How's your health? What the hell is wrong with you? What do you think? It's all about you? What kind of person are you? You were in my house 24/7 for over 36 years especially when my Dad went to work. You took advantage of that situation didn't you? I know what you were doing because I was awake. You can deny it all you FUCKING WANT but we both know what really happened. I wrote about it in my book, but to spare my mother's heart, I took it out.

I just might change my mind and rewrite this experience back in my book to make sure myself that you get it back in your face a million times over.

Sincerely your most favorite niece,
Gail Sanfilippo

P.S. You're in hell already! Bye, bye...

Gail,

I'm so sorry to have offended you. I usually don't write emails because im so slow typing I loose my trend of thought. I have spent time in hospital because I had nervous breakdowns trying to deal with my stupid mistakes and I am in hell as long as im alive. You were a person who I loved as much as anyone and were my favorite in all the world. Im am so sorry and im having trying to change the past and its impossible I dont blame you for hating me. I hate myself and I have for a long time.

This is OVER. I don't want to lay eyes on you ever again, even in your casket. It's ALL about you. You can't even apologize to your niece. It's what and how you felt and feel.

Goodbye, Uncle Jr.
Gail

Gail , I dont want to belabor the point but I was 18 years old . I know because I went into the army after that and I was 19 when I did. Uncle Jr.

First, you weren't 18 yrs. old, because that would make me 8 yrs. old and at that age I didn't or wouldn't had realized that stuff. If you can focus on anyone else besides yourself, I was going back and forth to Crotched Mountain for schooling and therapy. I was going through my own hell then having enemas stuck up me every day if I didn't take a shit or sleeping in a dorm with no curtains whatsoever hiding under bed covers from severe thunderstorms or the evils of life. What you did, we both will have to deal with, and it will take me time. Even though I knew I was right, after all these years finally having it being admitted brings it all back like a fresh cut. You're still my uncle, and I'm glad you admitted it. Now I need to process it. How you feel is up to you, not me.

Second, we are all our own worst enemies, Uncle Jr. Just look at your life, job, etc It isn't a pretty picture.

This will take time.....

Love,

G

Gail , I havent slept since I read your email. I want to tell you I was only 18 years old and it has caused me serious emotional problems that took me 20 years to deal with. I have tried to make amends in my personel life by doing the right things for all of my family I mean all. I was 18 and now Im going to be 65 in 4 months. It bothers me that you hate me. I always loved you as much as any one in my life. I felt hate for myself and had nervous breakdowns that I was hospitalized for. Were you trying to set me up? You told me I'm a fucking asshole because I didnt send you personal emails? You waited all these years for the right time to tell me I was a fucking asshole? You bring back feelings that I thought I dealt with years ago and you want to blow the situation up again? How ironic that you have the power to be the instrument of my destruction. I don't know how to sign this.

uncle Jr.

I have a single request of you. Please don't let me hear that you are calling my Mother for validation again. She told me the other day out of a conversation we were having. The problem that I'm having you are admitting and she is denying EVERYTHING...

I think it's quite funny how the two people who I love so much, besides my Dad, could have entirely DIFFERENT stories!

No more lies..............

G

On Sunday, January 27 2008 I finally knew it was not just in my head, but how do I live with this terrible reality and secret? I guess the realization that it was not my imagination and that my Uncle Junior is dying within himself is somewhat of a consolation.

Gail , What are talking about? Your mother didn't do anything. I was very drunk and made strong advances and she handled the situation without telling anybody so it didn't blow the world up for everybody. It was one of the worst things I ever did and was very shamed and emotionally distraught. I stopped going down the house after that like I was. I was terribly wrong and your mother is an honorable person who defused the situation and handled it with dignity.

Uncle Jr.

When I was about eight or nine years old, my Uncle Junior signed up for the Army Reserve in New Jersey. I remember him writing letters to me every couple of weeks. I do not believe he liked being away from his home and family although he always wrote about how well he was doing.

My Auntie Lilly was fourteen years older than me and was just like a big sister. She helped my mother a lot, especially nights, because I was so cranky from being hungry. She told me years later on how she and my mother took turns walking back and forth with me night after night. The few nights my father was home, he often had to go for walks around the block just to get away from my howling.

A couple years later, before she was married, Aunt Lilly carried me upstairs to her bedroom in front of my grandparents' apartment. She used to play dress up with me, using her old clothes. After she had her bridal shower she showed me all her gifts. When her children ware born she used to lay them on my wheelchair tray so I could play pica boo with them. I can still hear their giggles in my mind. Now they are all men over the age of forty-five.

Aunt Lilly's husband, James (who we called Uncle Sonny) passed away in late winter of 2004 of cancer.

Uncle Sonny owned a bar in Everett, and eventually started hitting the bottle too much himself. This was in the 1970s, and it was around this time that my Aunt started to immerse her whole life in religion. I guess it was her only answer for inner peace. During the 80s and 90s she became a real advocate for the Catholic faith, giving out Holy Communion in nursing homes and churches . I still have no idea how she was able to fill the role of clergy because she never was a nun as far as I know. Then again in my family, anything is possible. I shall never forget the time when my father and I were sitting in the kitchen when in walked Aunt Lilly with some holy water which she proceeded to sprinkle on the top of his head after his first heart attack. Thank God I was able to keep my composure and not burst out laughing! After that my Uncle Sonny sold the bar and started his new job with the United States government.

My Uncle Tony and Aunt Anna met when he traveled to Italy and they were married there. I still remember meeting her for the first time, when she presented me with a gold ring and said in broken English: "Uncle Tony told me all about you, Gail!" Aunt Anna could not speak English that well, but she was attractive girl with brownish hair and seemed to be very witty. Their daughter, Anna Maria, traveled as my Personal Care Attendant on a trip to Switzerland in the late 1980's. What fun we had! We were about to land when I felt so sick. I did not know that it was due to migraine headaches at the time, but when we landed people like Loring, the coordinator of many of our trips, just looked at me and said "You look green, Gail!" in his joking manner. When he saw that I wasn't laughing at his wise ass remark, he knew I was feeling quite ill. Since I told him I felt like I was going to be sick right there, I was one of the first passengers off the plane and my cousin took me to the nearest bathroom in the airport.

Thank God the sink was low enough to put my head over because, oh boy, was I sick. That night when we reached Mt. Rigi Kulm Hotel I went right to bed and slept for twelve hours straight.

It wasn't until the next morning that I could appreciate this whole experience. All around me I was encircled by puffy white clouds which were below the hotel's position on the mountain. If I didn't know I was still alive would had thought that I died and went to heaven. Yes, it was that picturesque and breath-taking! We were actually above the clouds and the horizon. I can still remember and saying to myself "I wonder if this looks like heaven?"

Then my wheelchair moved and I was literary being carried up to the back of the hotel to the highest peak by Ben. Now that was indescribable! As far as the eye can see there were mountains and light wispy clouds in every direction you looked. Yes, this was heaven.

My favorite remembrances with my Cousin Anna Maria are the times she fell asleep at a moment's notice. I still tease her about the time we were halfway down the Lucerne River and she woke up from a snooze, missing almost the whole tour. Whenever we get together nowadays we still talk about how we almost killed another woman named Carol when all of a sudden her wheelchair was rolling in the busy street in downtown Lucerne while Ben, Anne Marie, Roger, Lloyd and Sue were window shopping! And, of course, there was the scene at the airport when we were going through customs and my cousin was carrying pounds and pounds of Swiss chocolate, which we found out later was sold here in America, and two clocks!

Anna Maria never got married and is presently a Registered Nurse in one of the big hospitals in Boston.

Finally, there is my Aunt Josie. She has two daughters, Kathy and Terry, from her first marriage and one son by her second marriage. Kathy and Terry were like sisters to my sister Nancy and I when we were growing up on Vine Street in Everett. We were inseparable and they were always over when their dad went to work for days on the fishing boat. I fondly remember playing makeup and dress-up with our Barbie dolls for hours on end. Kathy and Terry were two sisters as different as night and day.

Kathy and Terry's father died in1967 . He was hit by a car driven by a drunk driver while he was crossing Broadway in Everett. After midnight, he had gone to purchase a sandwich in a nearby sub shop after a long night of drinking, which he often did after he got off the boat. My father had been working the graveyard shift that night at the Everett Police Department. I was lying awake in my bed when I heard him come into the house. I knew immediately something must be terribly wrong because he never came home before his shift ended. I heard my mother get out of bed to find out why he was home at two thirty in the morning. My mother, her voice raised in a state of alarm, ran to him and I heard her ask him why his face was as white as a sheet. He told my mother that his brother-in-law, my Uncle Mac, had been hit by a car and been taken to the hospital by ambulance. The next thing I heard were the frantic and worried voices of Kathy and Terry. Because my Aunt was being driven to the hospital, someone had brought my cousins to our house. In the darkness of my room I sensed how the mood throughout the house had changed from the quiet peace of an otherwise normal night to one of tearful and tragic wails.

As the days turned into weeks and family members prayed that my Uncle Mac would come out of his coma and off of life support, something told me, even at the age of thirteen, that if he did wake up, he would not be the same Uncle Mac I had known before this happened to him. It disturbed me so very much, because just weeks before I had seen him upstairs at my Nana's and had taken a mental note at how handsome my Uncle Mac was. After her father died, Terry and I became closer. One could assume that Terry and I were going through our own hells together but nobody could tell just by looking at us. Her mother, Aunt Josie, was always emotionally distant as far back as I can remember and was not able to deliver the comfort and compassion which Terry very much needed. She had to keep her feelings of grief bottled up deep inside and I felt bad for her because I knew how much she missed her beloved dad. I was often able to enjoy her laughter when we played together but as the years wore on Terry discovered her own brand of entertainment. She started drinking and all of her self respect vanished. Her world became a circus of men, liquor and promiscuity.

In time, Terry became the thing she hated, an alcoholic. In April of 1999 she left behind four lovely daughters after her drug overdose suicide. It left the rest of her relatives to wonder "Why???"

As we got older, Kathy went her own way too, and I was alone again. I shall never forget when she walked right passed me with one of her boyfriends in the driveway between the houses where we lived. My Mom saw it all, thank God, and said some choice words to her from our kitchen window! It was not until after she got married in her mid 20s that she started to acknowledge me as her cousin again, inviting me over to her apartment and sometimes going out to see what the night life was all about. More than a few times, it was not a pretty picture when we ventured out on the town. One night in particular was a really hair raising experience. We were headed out of Everett Square for a night of partying when the car in front of us came to a sudden stop. Kathy had to slam on the brakes and I nearly went through the dashboard of my blue van. My wheelchair had not been secured previous to the start of our trip. My chair went flying and my nose smashed against the console and started to bleed profusely. Kathy was screaming hysterically and wanted to take me to the hospital. I would have no part of it and was not going to let a smashed and bloody nose get in the way of my night out. The first club we went into was filled with other patrons and before we could say "Give me a shot and make it a double" drinks were being bought for us. We had a variety of cocktails I have never seen the likes of since. Then we went to a Revere night club and asked for some ice for my swollen nose and eye. I actually do not remember when I arrived home to face the music from my mother.

Maybe it was better that I did not commit this to memory! If I did get a lecture, I sure as hell do not remember. I was feeling no pain!

Another time was when someone was going to get married and the bridesmaids took her out one evening before her big day. As we went bar hopping, we ran into this guy named Harry. Well, dear Harry made a pass at me, of all individuals, and asked if he could fuck me as a favor. He said he had a friend with Multiple Sclerosis and does her this favor. Let me only say that after this came out of his mouth, all seven of us girls went into a fit of laughter. When I composed myself in a few minutes, I said to him: "You have balls and, by the way, I already have a boyfriend!"

After Uncle Mac died and Terry and I got closer, my sister and I slowly grew apart when my parents gave her a little freedom when she turned 14. I can admit now, forty years later, that I was jealous of her being able to go out at night, but she had to be home at a certain time. I'm not sure whether my parents just didn't see it or chose to ignore the fact that 90% of the time she came home either high as a kite from marijuana or smelled like alcohol. This I knew, because we slept in the same bedroom together for about eight years. And why shouldn't she get away with it? She was always considered as the good and quiet daughter in my mother's eyes. Our mother never realized that my sister was afraid of her when she was growing up. My sister finally got away from this fear when she got married at the young age of 21, but this freedom could only last for so long. After she gave birth to her second child, Lindy, in 1984 her husband, Steve, could not pay the rent on their apartment so they had to come back and live in one of my parents' houses adjacent to Vine Street. Her escape was in vain because of my ex brother-in-law's drinking problem , although Steve was never a bad guy. He just drank his six pack of beer every night but, as years went on his habit became more serious when he begun drinking the hard stuff and not giving my sister money for food and bills when they moved to Danvers in 1990's. When I came home from my apartment each week for a couple of days to be with my Mother and give my attendant at this time some time off for her own life, I noticed my sister simply avoiding the whole situation. She took a couple of jobs as a pizza waitress and as a bartender on Thursday, Friday and Saturday nights.

She was avoiding her reality just like when she got married at 21, thinking she would be getting her freedom and chance to go out at night with her coworkers without having to answer to anyone. But her freedom only lasted until she got pregnant with Lindy and it was then that she was finally told by my mom that she could not possibly look after two babies along with caring for me. It was then that my sister became reliant on my parents again and is to this very day.

So, the beat goes on. My sister is still under my mother's roof in a newly renovated apartment with her second husband, whom she dotes on. She has no time for anyone but him, except sometimes my mother when she gets an asthma attack and a friend or two at work. I'll never forget about four years back when I was short on my Personal Care help and my Mom was away for a week on a cruise. I'd asked my sister if she could possibly come by on her way home from work just in case I needed to go to the toilet or have a cup of tea. She simply said on the phone: "No. This week I'm going to have the whole house to myself with my husband." As I pressed the speaker button off with my head stick, I cursed her and wished she was in this wheelchair with her arms and feet tied together, at the mercy of others for her daily survival. How would she deal with my reality? How far would she have gotten in her life? Not too far, I am afraid to say. I can honestly pick out a lot of individuals who I am sure could never live my life of having to completely depend on others for 98% of their daily activities and physical needs. Two of them are my own siblings, Frank and Nancy. Another is Ed's father, who no matter what his body is telling him just ignores the doctor and his aches and pains and goes on practicing or playing his weekly tennis games, injuring his knees and hip over and over again. But in the end who suffers more except the caregivers?

PART TWO

MY FREEDOM

CHAPTER 8

MY LOVES

The road to freedom came in 1985. The price of freedom involved making maximum use of my knowledge and past experience while trying to make up for my complete inexpert-ience with dating or living on my own.

Five years earlier I placed my name on the waiting list at Ocean Shores Apartments on the Lynnway. When I received a call from my former girlfriend, Brenda, saying an apartment had become available I was both very excited and somewhat scared.

In between the negative comments and the guilt trips from my Mother over moving out, my sister and I went to see the apartment. My Mother had this ill-conceived notion that my sister would be taking care of me whenever the time came when she could not do it any longer. Myself, having to live with reality whether I liked to or not, knew my sister had all she could do to take care of herself much less a disabled sister.

Although the apartment was very small, I felt I was finally free to do what I wanted when I wanted or nothing at all if I choose to do nothing. The apartment consisted only of three rooms, a kitchen , a combined living/dining room and a bedroom. I had been dreaming about my freedom for so long that I had saved for years with my government checks as my only source of income. I was more than ready to live on my own. I was at the threshold of experiencing new things. My new life called out to me and beckoned me closer. I was free at last, free at last! The nightlife awaited me along with the parties, the boyfriends (most of who turned out to be assholes) and all the new people I would meet, of which today only a handful still remain in my life.

It was not until I got my own apartment that I began dating at the ripe old age of thirty-three!

My first experience was not very good. In fact, it was TERRIBLE. The guy turned out to have a ton of baggage from his childhood. I guess his father used to beat him. So, I guess he took it out on me in some way or another. The verbal abuse was constant, not to mention the head games he played on me. I soon came to realize he was still stuck in his past with his own unresolved problems and I was getting the brunt of it. I hated him and knew I had to get rid of him, but at the same time I had illusions that I was able to help him. As each weekend approached, I wondered what the hell he was going to pull out of his sick mind. As days turned into weeks, and weeks into months, my uneasiness grew into fear. My fear began after watching "9 ½ Weeks" the 1986 movie with actress Kim Basinger and actor Mickey Rourke about their relationship of nine and a half weeks falling to pieces. Fifteen minutes into the movie, anyone can realize that he is using her for his own sick need to control and dominate another person's life because his own has been shattered and destroyed.

As the months moved on, I realized I was a pawn in Bob's life, a weak and convenient person on whom he could out take out his frustration and resentment. And so he did just that. The smallest things set him off into a tirade for minutes or hours. If this sounds like a poor excuse for a man, it was. His dislike for peas or a song which came on the radio would enraged him to a point where he would yell or mumble on and on. I knew he was a freak, a total nut, yet I took it in stride due to my naiveté at the time. One night I asked him after a few drinks "Why are you with me?" He replied, "I'm going to make you walk." I just sat there not knowing what to say or do. I was completely astounded and afraid knowing that, in time, this man had to go. Right then and there I knew he was completely nuts and was just with me to use me for a place to crash. He also wanted to take advantage of weekends in a comfortable apartment. I came to this conclusion when my sister and brother-in-law, Steve, invited Bob and I over to their apartment to see a Woody Allen movie. During the movie, a joint was passed around, and he walked out. So what if he was against it? How dare he preach morality at the same time he was treating me like shit? My sister said he must be in the bathroom, but when twenty minutes elapsed and he did not come back, I asked my brother-in-law to find out what happened to him. Sure enough he was in the bathroom like a little boy, throwing a temper tantrum when he doesn't get his own way, pouting and stewing because he didn't approve of me smoking. If he had acted in a mature manner, he would have left our lines of communication open and realized that I did not get a damn thing out of smoking and was just experimenting with it. I have never bothered with it since then, but that was not the point.

It took a couple of more months for me to get up the nerve to confront him. So with my aide with me for support I laid the question to him again, "Why the hell are you with me?" I knew damn well he did not love or care about me. He threw a crazy fit and started trashing my apartment. This guy needed men in little white coats to take him away. Luckily, I had asked my attendant to stay that night, because somehow I knew something was going to happen. After he calmed down, he just slept on the couch and went home to New Hampshire in the morning without any answers or goodbyes. Today, knowing what I know now, I would have done things differently and the police would have been escorting him out of my life!

The last time I saw him was down the Cape at my parents' cottage two and a half months after my Dad's death because I stupidly invited him. I just want to forget those two days that seemed like two weeks. To this day I feel so much rage at his behavior when we were a so called couple that I will feel it for the rest of my life. I now know, from this life experience with him, what hate feels like. It is a real feeling regardless of how painful it is to accept. At the Cape, the first thing which came out of his mouth was "Where are the lobsters?" He never even had the manners to ask me "How are you doing, Gail?" as he was served chicken cutlets, I had to leave the kitchen in complete disgust. The agony I had to endure because of his late arrival, his assumption about having lobster for dinner and his total disregard over my Dad's sudden death two months earlier, and embarrassing me in front of my family had me clothed in red!

The second and third day was no better. I found out he came up from Pennsylvania with only thirty dollars, so I unreasonably threw some of my money at him to get him the hell out of Dodge. He meandered down to Provincetown to look for a woodworking job. Then came the second day, which was even worse. We all went to the beach, my Mom, sister with two small children, Bob and me. Speaking of wet blankets, he cast a cloud over the whole day with his pessimistic remarks. He hated everything. Little did he realize I despised him by this time. That night I refused to leave the kitchen as I, in no way, wanted to be in the same room with him. The balls on this man were unbelievable. He had the audacity to stretch his sorry ass out on the couch as if to say, "Deal with me." Although my sister and I have our differences, she was a true ally to me this time. She knew how I was feeling and backed me up the whole night. She broke out the Scrabble and the Captain Morgan and made my evening tolerable, bless her heart. When it came to be after eleven o'clock, my sister pushed my chair to the living room so I could say that I was going to bed and say my goodbyes. I knew he was leaving at 5 am the next morning and had the fantasy that he would beat around the bush during our goodbyes. What a foolish notion that was. Reality sucks, yet is the cold hard truth. That night I learned a valuable life lesson. I was hurt but not heartbroken. My sister came to my defense saying to Bob "What don't you understand? I'm in the other room and can hear my sister as clear as day!" She went on with other choice words, but he did not move at all.

After that, all I remember is my Mother playing psychologist until two in the morning and my sister coming to the bedroom with a knife, placing it right at arm's reach under the mattress. My Mother, my sister and I got no sleep that night. Of course Bob slept like a baby. At approximately half past five, the hell ended. As he got up, went into the bathroom and gathered his things together, I could hear my Mother going to the refrigerator to get food. Little did I know then she had made two sandwiches for this idiot for his ride back home.

In November 1989, I met Andy. He was this man of over six feet four inches tall and looked like a typical lumber jack with his long grayish beard, but was actually a high school teacher from Vermont. Being an educated man, he was a real gentleman towards me. It was kind of funny when we went out together, because we looked like Mutt and Jeff due to his height and me, a hundred pound skeleton in a wheelchair. It was like looking up at a giant. Andy was my first partner in love making.

I will always remember the events leading up to it that night. We had gone out to the Elks in Marblehead with my attendant, Jackie, and her boyfriend, Steve. As they were playing several games of pool, Andy and I were just chit chatting. Suddenly, he asked me if he could inquire about something and if I did not wish to answer it was perfectly fine. In a quiet and gentle way he asked if I ever had intercourse before. I said, "No. Does that bother you?" He said "No, of course not."

99

That night as intended, he stayed, because I did not want him to drive home at that late hour of the night. My attendant got me ready and put me on the love seat so Andy could sleep on the sofa bed which pulled out. When we got settled in, we just talked for quite awhile. I can still hear him saying to me "You look very uncomfortable on that small sofa." I tried very hard to convince him that I was not uncomfortable but that did not work very well. Soon I was carried to the sofa couch in his arms. He touched and caressed me in ways I had never experienced before. I just remember how it felt so right and good. Yes, it was a wonderful experience because he was the right guy at that time.

I went to my gynecologist soon after to get on the pill. What an experience that was! He asked me "Why?" as his nurse, who was a plump woman in her sixties, almost keeled over. I said to the so called, educated man, "I like taking pills!" You can bet I never went back to him again!

When my male gynecologist took this attitude, I found a woman doctor. The only problem I had was that all of her patients were welfare clients and minorities. I keep on forgetting that I am considered a minority, too. While sitting in the waiting room, I kept on saying in my head "I'm only disabled and without a job because nobody would hire me due to my disability and appearance." Along with this, I realized they probably were looking at me, thinking "Why is this cripple woman here seeing a gynecologist? She couldn't possibility have any connection with a man, nevertheless have sex!"

When I met the woman doctor, I was more at ease. After a pap test, I talked to her about my first experience and why did it hurt somewhat. She smiled and sat down with me, saying "It isn't you, Gail. The first time is always difficult for 95% of all women but it isn't talked about often. Maybe it is the angle he's putting it in you!" The funny thing was she was not making a joke. I found out that she was right as the weeks and months went by!!!

My very first gynecologist exam was when I was about thirty years old and it was the worse experience I ever had in my life. It was at the Beth Israel Hospital in Boston and my sister went with me. After the long and dragged out stay in the waiting room I was finally called to go to an exam room , in which I lingered for another forty-five minutes. Then the hell began. On to the exam slab I saw two doctors on either side of me, not including my sister. Of course they asked my sister if I ever had a pap test prior and if I was sexually active. "No" she replied after questioning me. Then my most painful examination begun, as they inserted the cold speculum in my vagina I thought I was going to die. The pain was so bad. I found out afterward that they used a speculum applied normally on women who were previously pregnant.

Another guy who I met was a fly by night event. I met him at a bar and he asked me to go out with him one night for dinner. He had a slight case of Cerebral Palsy that affected his speech and walk to some extent. He was a big, heavily built man who had a little bit of weight on him.

I refused his invitation very politely, telling him that I do not just go out with men I do not know. But in return, I asked him over to my apartment while my Personal Care Attendant would be there. As we talked and took the elevator down to the entertainment area just to talk, he told me he just broke up with his girlfriend who was pregnant with his child. I could just look intently at him in utter disbelief. My heart was breaking once more because he hadn't told me the truth from the very beginning. He made me think he was single and carefree. I really liked this guy , maybe because Paul reminded me of my Dad with a large, robust frame and a jovial outlook. I foolishly asked him if he was going back to the girlfriend. To this day, I do not know why.

I did see him one more time and made a complete fool out of myself, saying I did not care whether he had a girlfriend/wife. Oh, what we do for companionship and so-called love…….

In 1990, John came into my life. We had been writing back and forth for a short time but never made plans to meet. Surprisingly we met at a Boston Center For Independent Living group session called "Disability and Sexuality." Prior to the meeting, I felt someone watching me from across the room. All of a sudden, he rode over to me in his electric chair and asked "Are you Gail?" As I said "Yes" I had no idea who the hell this guy was! I guess he'd seen this look all over my face and introduced himself quickly. After the introductions, we were soon called into another room for the seminar. From then on all I remember is that he sat on my left and kept looking over at me. He had this infectious smile whenever I saw him glancing at me and he thought I was not looking. But he knew that I saw his every gesture by the grin on my face.

It was his personality that captured me into a four year relationship. Reflecting upon this relationship, it was filled with every emotion contained in the word relationship: love, dislike, anger, mistrust, lies, truth, and fear.

John, having had Polio since he was five, was used to his daily lifestyle of ventilators, naps and respirators, but in time these things took control of his world. I thought that Cerebral Palsy was my monster but in time I realized that other individuals have bigger and more powerful ones. At least with my monster, I can go anywhere and anytime I wished. It wasn't the same for John. His days were controlled by his lungs and body strength. The only deviation from his schedule was when I came into the equation. Sundays and Thursdays I forced him out of his rut. Every Sunday my Mother and Auntie Joan drove me the 22 miles from Everett to Randolph to drop me off at his house where we had a simple turkey sandwich from the nearby deli or went out to eat. Our favorite restaurant was Phillip's Old Colony House in Boston on Morrissey Blvd. The establishment was also a venue for parties and weddings so at times, wherever we were seated, we could see all of the events. The restaurant had its own sophistication, from the décor of past decades to the unique food that was served.

Six months down the road, his stroke added another element of life. Since his Mother and his spinster sister prohibited me from visiting him in the hospital, bitterness engulfed me. This lasted for just a week until I got into reality mode. Who in the hell were they or anyone else to keep me from seeing my boyfriend? Yes, I was a little apprehensive in seeing John. Will he remember me? Remember my name? There were so many unknowns, but that's life. I did go to Massachusetts General Hospital about eight days after John's stroke, regardless of his Mother and sister's objections. I can still see in my mind the taken aback expressions on both their faces. They were in complete distress and dismay, especially the sister who actually kicked me out of the hospital room. When the sister realized I was not going anywhere, she walked her heavy built body out of the room.

When I saw John, he smiled in an awkward and strange way. In moments I found out that he did not remember my name, but recalled that he had a girlfriend. It was very difficult for me to place a smile on my face and keep my composure. Questions passed through my mind . Will he ever remember my name again? Will we ever have a relation-ship again?

Soon I would know. After he went into a rehabilitation hospital in Lakeville, Massachu-setts, which was about a forty mile ride from Everett, Massachusetts, John turned into a religious fanatic. John believed God was punishing him for his wrong doings in the last six months, so that stopped our sex life completely. John had changed. I was going out with a new man who I didn't know or like. Later after his release from Lakeville, I suggested that we go to couple counseling. The first counselor said after meeting with us that we were very well adjusted handicapped individuals. As we wheeled out of his office, we both looked at one another laughing hysterically. This was not the point at all. We just needed advice, or rather I required a suggestion as to why John had done a 180. We requested another counselor with more experience who worked with us and took it from there. Finally the truth came out about John's fear of God. John truly believed God punished him by having sex outside and inside of marriage. At last I knew why John had a complete transformation but the question was in the back of my mind: Could I live with it: Marriage with no sex? My instinct told me this was not normal. Soon I found out that this relationship was not between two people. It was all about John. The days he came over, he began telling me about the intimate things that happened with this female Personal Care Attendant, Julie. Oh, boy! She had him under her spell with the way she dressed. She was a tiny little thing with long russet hair which she usually tied back with an elastic band. She wore tight, short tops which showed her belly button. I got to see her as she started to drive John to my apartment once a week and I came to realize that she was swindling my man out of money for some kind of operation or whatever. First, she had to have an abortion and next she had cancer. Either one was so terrible in itself, but lying about either one made it even worse. On top of this, she had her own boyfriend. What a con artist she turned out to be.

As the months turned into years, I knew this relationship was not going anywhere. We broke up time and time again. I was hearing things which I did not want or need to hear such as how he got an erection while Julie was given him a bath, etc, etc. The final episode was when John was planning on coming for a full week visit to my apartment in September of 1994. He was only paying my attendants two hours of pay a day to help him through his morning lung exercises, his bathing and his bedtime setup of being put on his respirator which took at least an hour by itself. He ripped them off of at least seven hours a day.

This was the end. We talked on the phone every day for months, but we both knew it was all over. He wanted to turn me into a different person who held Bible studies every week. He wanted to have a platonic marriage and for me to be a subservient wife. Looking back, I am so pleased I walked away, or rather wheeled away!

Since then I have visited John with Ed who would become the love of my life.

As time passed, I just called to see how he was doing. I found out he got married and was living in a complex for the elderly and disabled. Our brief conversation was very hasty and rude. In the meantime, his wife, Debra, was making an asshole out of herself as I heard her inarticulate speech in the background.

The second time I called was to inquire about his mother whom I'd known for years. I heard bad news that John's older marred sister, Carolyn, had passed away from breast cancer, leaving behind two teen aged children. I didn't know what to say. She was such a nice person that I, in my mind, questioned God or whomever -Why?

The last time I called him was in April 26, 2006 to just inquire about his Mother. Well, he was most insulting, while his wife was screaming in the background once again. I did not say a word as John told me, "We had an understanding that you would not call again." Then my Personal Care Attendant, Joy, said he was just a hypocrite and John hung up.

Then my soul mate, Ed, came into my life. I met him via a dating service for both able and disabled individuals. We each wrote a brief introduction and were assigned a mailbox number. I wrote to two men and one of them was Ed. Although he was eleven years younger than me, I took a chance because from his letter it didn't seem like his disability was his whole life. It seemed he was coming from the same place as I was. Yes we were disabled but it did not swallow up our whole existence.

The letters and phone calls between us came regularly. With him residing in Medfield and myself in Lynn, we kept Verizon in business!

Our first official date was on June 2, 1995 at the Marriott in Woburn and from then on I began writing a journal because I just knew Ed was the one....

As my attendant drove me there, I was so nervous. Although I told Ed all about myself, this meeting was for real. What if my disability turned him off? What about my speech? What if??? As we drove into the parking lot of the Marriott, it did not look full. Was this the right place? I asked my Personal Care Attendant to go in before she got me out of my van to check if Ed was there. As she was walking inside, Ed was coming out. It was that close. She asked him if he was Ed and the rest was history. We went across the highway to the Radisson, had a few drinks and tried to talk over the deafening noise of a juke box. I honestly thought it was going to be a disaster, especially with my difficulty with speech anyways, but all seemed to go okay because Ed asked me out again, this time to dinner at Jimmy's Restaurant at Burlington Mall.

The date at the restaurant was much better. I will always remember the hostess in the lounge saying "There isn't any room in the lounge," while we were overlooking tables that were fully unoccupied. This was discrimination at its best. Before I fully came to my senses, Ed began moving furniture around, making room for my wheelchair at one of the tables. As the hostess just stood there in shock and disbelief we settled down and ordered our drinks. The rest of the night went perfect. We talked and ate in ease. As we left the restaurant, going to my van, he bent over to kiss me and asked me out to a picnic overlooking the Charles River the next Saturday. Of course I said "Yes."

The Charles River was beautiful but someone must have made a mistake in preparing the Kentucky Fried Chicken that I had bought. It was so salty that we got feeling very, very thirsty after we gulped our beverages of beer and pineapple juice/rum drinks. We started kissing like nobody was around and did not care.

For our next date he came to my apartment for the weekend at the end June. We went down the street to a place called Porthole Restaurant to eat, have a couple of drinks and listen to Karaoke. This was our regular agenda for just about every weekend, including watching rental movies such as Temptation, Walk In The Clouds and a few porno videos.

On one of Ed's vacation days in August 1995, he unexpectedly invited me to his parents' home. I was so uncomfortable at first, especially with my speech impairment, but it all went well after every one relaxed. As I was going through this uncomfortable incident, Ed disappeared. I was going to kill him later that evening. He just left me in a very agonizing situation. His answer that he gave me later that night was, "I just wanted Dad and Mom to get to know you." After I smacked him a few times on his arm we both just laughed.

I recall that August afternoon perfectly. It was a sunny day in the mid 70s, but I could feel the sweat rolling down my back because of my nerves. Ed's Mom, Jane, was very attractive with short, blond hair. I could quickly tell she was a lady with class by the way she conducted herself and by the way she carried herself in this most stressful event. This was the first time her son had invited a girl home in his entire life!

Ed's Dad, Edward Sr., was a handsome, well fit man who had on a tee shirt, shorts and sneakers, his usual attire on summer days as I quickly discovered. He did not say much, but I knew what was going through his mind. I know he must have felt a little uncertain about his son's choice to go out with a totally disabled woman.

The hardest part about this meeting was my speech impairment and Ed leaving me alone to deal with it with his parents. Combined with nerves, I did not do well at all.

August almost brought another surprise into my life. I was two weeks late with my period, so I truly believed I was pregnant because I was like clock work. All I thought about was my Mother. I could already see her face even before I told her. My sister was supposed to help me take the pregnancy test but she had to go to work that night so it was clear that my Mother had to. This was another inconvenience about being disabled , nothing is private. That night was the longest night of my life. My aunt and uncle came to visit and did not go home until one thirty in the morning. In the meantime, I was gulping glasses of water and tea making sure I was able to pee when they left. By the time midnight came my bladder felt like it was going to rupture. Another hour and a half ticked by, and I suffered both physically and emotionally. What if I was pregnant? Would Ed leave me? How would I take care of a baby anyway? I could not even go to the bathroom by myself. Around two o'clock, I knew my fate. After I peed onto the pregnancy stick, I had to wait another five minutes for the results, which felt like hours. I was not pregnant, thank God. Although it was a big relief, inside I felt emptiness. Some-thing died in me in a way. Ed was disappointed because he'd wanted me to be pregnant and get married.

As our dating continued, Ed met my Mother and family. Each holiday we took turns to visit both of our parents' or Ed's uncle and aunt's homes. I especially remember that Thanksgiving when I met his Grandmother Fran. She was so uncomfortable around me. It is so funny how the different generations look upon a disabled person but this was her loss. She never gave me a chance.

The major holidays where all of Ed's uncles, aunts and cousins get together are Memorial Day, July 4th and Labor Day either at his parents' home in Kingston or one of his cousin's homes. Ed's family is quite a large family and very close, and I am very lucky to have them. His mother and father especially have a great sense of humor and kind, understanding hearts.

However as it goes, there were exceptions to the rule. As the years traveled by, I soon saw flaws. One of them was favoritism toward the grandchildren. I couldn't give them grandchildren due to my age. It came into sight especially at Christmas time when Ed's mother held down the holiday tradition bringing the grandchildren to see the "Nutcracker" no matter what age they were. The remarkable truth was I had never seen the ballet even at 54 years old, but she's been dragging the grand kids to this occasion since they were four, year after year.

Another happening was when I broke my leg in Aruba and had to be specially flown back to a Boston hospital for six days. While my mother and Ed were taking turns staying at the hospital with me day and night, because of my speech, Ed's mother never even offered to stay one night with me to give her own son a decent night of rest. When confronted with her action she just ran out of my dining room with tears rolling down her face, because she couldn't take the "truth" or be rebuked in any shape or form.

As the months went on, Ed asked me if he could move in with me. My response was,

"Not until you make some kind of commitment." I guess it took him by surprise, but I got a ring on the day after Thanksgiving and went from there.

He moved into my already crowded three room apartment: a small kitchen, a combined dining-/-living room and a bedroom. I was simply appalled when his dad brought in these two gigantic stereo speakers that came from the 70s. As I looked at his father in absolute disbelief, he went into fits of laughter. I said "Take these monstrosities out of here! Where do you think you are going to put them anyway?"

We have been together for about eleven years now. Due to the outlandish laws on marital unions in America, we were never "legally" married.

CHAPTER 9

MAINE SWEET MAINE

In the summer of 2006 Ed and I traveled by car to Maine for a mini vacation. Doug Preston, one of my really good friends from my summer camp days, had made reservations at a lovely restaurant and was planning to meet Ed and I, along with Doug's wife, for dinner. It was really special to see him after such a long time and I was looking forward to it. From the sound of Doug's upbeat voice on a previous phone call he would be happy to see me also.

Situated right on the coast, Boothbay Harbor is a quaint little fishing community where the primary means of earning a living are trapping lobster, clam digging and deep sea fishing for cod, flounder, bluefish and haddock. This is where I booked a room for our trip. The waterfront was brimming with tourists. The fishermen were preparing to work on their boats and every morning at dawn I would watch the lights on boats going out to sea. At night those boats headed back to the harbor. It really energized our spirits as we sat on our small patio, cocktail in hand, playing scrabble and watching the beautiful sun setting over the old weather beaten docks. The Capt 'n Fish Motel reserved us a room right on the pier. I always make sure when I am making my reservations that the shower stall is wheelchair accessible, but apparently who ever took my reservation had no clue what a disabled person's bathroom looked like. The bathroom did not come up to par by ADA laws; it was barely adequate. The shower had a six inch lip on it which deterred Ed from just placing me in my shower chair. Instead, he had to think of his own safety as well as mine by putting one foot into the shower stall and the other on the bathroom floor, thus keeping his leverage while carrying me in his arms. The sink was small and positioned in the original tiny crook where the builders had put it when the building was first built. It took a lot of maneuvering to get to. It is unfortunate that we are in the twenty first century now and still such ignorance exists in the United States in that I am not able to find handicapped accessible bathroom facilities no matter where I travel.

The next morning, we awoke to a glorious sunrise. It was a sight for sore eyes, truly idyllic. Ed left to grab a bite for his breakfast and then we decided to check out the downtown area. To our chagrin, ninety-eight percent of the shops and restaurants were not accessible at all to the elderly or the disabled. The only handicapped accessible

building was the old fashioned stationary store, which was strange since it is now the age of computers and emails. There were stairs and hilly sidewalks everywhere we wanted to go, but we could not due to the town's commitment to preserving the old historic buildings and homes. What would it take to put concrete ramps with railings on the sides of buildings since the average citizen is living a lot longer compared to centuries ago? It was awful because I was not able to go into any of the little shops that tourists take for granted on vacation, nor were Ed and I able to get a bite to eat in any of the downtown restaurants. This was the downside of our trip to Boothbay Harbor as has been the downside of many a trip for us. It seems that society and government takes care of everyone but the disabled and, if things do not change quickly, there are going to be a lot of baby boomers up in arms as they age and need more handicapped accessibility options to keep their independence. This baby boomer generation and our disabled citizens of the country, after years of being ignored, are at the threshold of demanding their needs be met.

As Ed and I contemplated what we were going to do for the day, we just drove and drove along the winding streets and back roads. We found ourselves in the woods beyond Boothbay Harbor and looked at each other wondering where the hell we were. It is easy to get lost in those dense woods. Since we were headed towards the vicinity of the restaurant that we were going to for dinner the next evening with Doug and his wife, we decided to take a trial run. Thank God we did because we would never have found it otherwise. It was in the middle of nowhere on an unpaved dirt road, a TOTALLY different route than Doug had told us over the phone that morning. I did not even know what township we were traveling to. It was like being in a maze of dirt roads with side paths beaten down by November's hunters. Only by asking directions did we get there. Doug's well laid directions left something to be desired! The Newagen Seaside Inn, poised on the tip of Cape Newagen in Southport, was simply charming, reminding me of one of my favorite author's book, F. Scott Fitzgerald's novel "The Great Gatsby" which was written in 1925 prior to the Great

Depression. The lush expansive lawn reminded me of the setting where gentlemen in their top hats and slicked backed hair drank scotch, while nonchalantly eyeing the ladies who were milling about in their flapper dresses, drinking mint juleps in the shade of an old oak tree.

The same afternoon I suggested to Ed that we drive to my friend Doug's house because my curiosity streak was getting the best of me. I was dying to know what kind of home a famous author like my friend was living in. After driving around in circles with only the bears to ask directions from, we came across a small white building that turned out to be the Round Pond Post Office. I had to literally beg Ed to go in and ask directions to the Preston residence. If I had left it up to him I would still be up there shitting with the bears in the woods. The Postmaster, without a second thought, told Ed where the Preston residence was. (Gee, they are trusting in those parts!) Up the road AGAIN we went looking for this small sign with the name of "Preston" on it. A short path down the road I saw his sign. We made a left turn into what seemed to be this dirt road in the middle of the woods that went on for MILES and MILES. Doug's home is in a really isolated part of Maine. It was then that I knew how he was able to write science fiction novels and the horror stories for which he is so famous.

As we headed back to Boothbay Harbor after seeing where Doug lived, I wondered how people made a living there. Some folks seemed to be extremely well to do with their fancy yachts moored in the harbor but on the other hand we drove past small shacks that were scattered by the side of the roads. These small homes had peeling paint and shingles coming off the roofs where tarpaper was laid. Old rusty hubcaps, broken machinery, broken chairs and general debris littered the yards. Ancient pines hung over old doghouses like a giant umbrella.

Ed and I were hungry after driving around for hours so we decided to stop at this Chinese restaurant called China by the Sea, in Boothbay. As soon as we entered the establishment, I knew we were in for trouble by the look on the 40ish waitress's face. Because we were physically disabled she automatically assumed that we had a mental disability as well. That has ALWAYS been the story of my life and it is so damn insulting. No one should make such judgments based upon sight alone. I always wish I could put them in their place and show them my college diploma. Maybe I'll start carrying it with me when we go anywhere! Needless to say, it makes for a very unpleasant meal when this happens. We finally got our drinks, after being questioned on whether we wanted alcohol in them. This got me furious inside because my intelligence was being judged through my physical appearance. When the drinks did arrive they were so weak we had to send them back. We were not paying for damn fruit juice here! On top of that, another waitress butted in and said she would fix them. Oh she fixed them alright. They were no better than before. At least the food was delicious, although I was too upset to eat much. We left, brought it back to our motel room and ate it later.

Tuesday morning Ed got up early and went to breakfast while I stayed in bed waiting for him to come back with mine. We took it easy Tuesday as we were meeting Doug and his wife for dinner in the evening. It was wonderful just to lounge around and take in the salt air. The day before we had passed a Mexican restaurant called Tamales that had a ramp so we went there for a snack around two thirty that afternoon. We ordered tacos and they were fabulous. The drinks were excellent also and we were treated very well.

At a quarter past four another family came in and were seated next to us. I saw the look that they gave me {this comes with being disabled}, a look of distain and horror like I am a monster or had a transmittable disease. It is just unbelievable since they did not even know me. Anyway, they wanted to move to a different table and gave the waitress a lame excuse about having the sun in their faces. Ed and I left at this point and headed back to the motel room to get ready for the evening.

When we got to our room, Ed helped me freshen up and get dressed for the evening. My current attendant, Joy, had already taken good care of packing and had painstakingly folded the dress I was going to wear for our dinner date, so all Ed had to do was put it on me. Ed did a hell of a good job putting on my makeup for this special occasion because he knew that it really was special to me. We headed out to eat, confident that we would be there on time, after scouting it out the day before. When we arrived, we were seated at a table overlooking the expansive lawns on the shores of the Atlantic Ocean. Ed ordered a bottle of wine brought to the table, which we enjoyed until Doug and his wife showed up. I had been keeping an eye on the front door so I was not prepared when I heard Doug's voice coming from the direction of the back door when they arrived. Introductions were made all around, which flowed into pleasant conversation between the four of us. It was obvious to the other diners how much of a good time we were having as I caught them looking over at us. The food was extraordinary and we were in no rush to finish as we were enjoying each other's company so much. Doug ordered a fabulous dessert of bananas foster which I had never had before. After dinner, we all walked down towards the water. We could not have asked for a better night. I have seen many stars twinkling in the sky when I was young and vacationed down in Cape Cod, but this was special. As Ed and Doug's wife, Christine, conversed at the steps to the pier, Doug wheeled me across the rough terrain and onto the end of the pier. We commented to each other how beautiful the scenery was around us. The light of the full moon cast a ribbon of diamonds on the ocean. There was this one particular house on the water that I absolutely loved. I told Doug that if I lived there I'd never want to leave. We began talking about how hard it is to write a book surrounded by the distractions of daily living. He understood what I was going through as I continued work on my own book. Christine and Doug walked back to the car with Ed and me. As Ed and I drove away, I felt so good that after all these years my feelings for Doug have turned into a true and valuable friendship that will last my lifetime.

Wednesday morning Ed got up early and walked to breakfast at the motel's restaurant, which was a stone's throw away from our room. He brought back a couple of sausages for me because I had to have something in my stomach to start the day. They looked like last night's leftovers and they tasted like it too! We packed and headed to Doug and Christine's house for a visit. As Ed wheeled me to the van, I looked around at the gorgeous scenery that I was leaving behind, questioning myself if I would ever be here again. It was so peaceful and serene but yet so alive with activity.

The drive to Doug and Christine's house was easier since Ed and I had ventured up to the area on Monday. The ride seemed to be shorter this time, maybe because we knew where we were going. I speculated on how people could live in this isolated place so far away from civilization. Supermarkets, hospitals and the general public were an hour or more away.

When Ed and I got there, Christine was outside watering her plants and came right over when she saw the van. Doug came out of the house and after Ed helped me out of the van, Doug maneuvered me in my wheelchair up the three steps to the door. It was funny because Doug said that he hoped he still remembered how to lift me up the stairs. We all sat around and talked in the living room while Christine brought out ice tea, fruit and cookies. They showed us pictures of Italy from when they used to live there. We left around one thirty because Ed and I had a long ride to Massachusetts.

Our second vacation to Boothbay Harbor, Maine in September of '07 took on new meaning. That is to say, what we expected never came true. Or did it? After Ed checked us into the Rocktide Inn, which was on the same street as the Capt 'n Fish Motel, he got my wheelchair's tiedowns unlashed which is a task in itself. This invention has four canvas straps with hooks on either end that secure my wheelchair in the van while driving. This particular design was created by someone who either had no clue about wheelchairs or had a lot of time on his hands. This elaborate system of tie down points and tension locks requires an advanced degree in engineering to operate efficiently. After a four minute workout to remove my lockdowns, Ed sped me over to the nearest entrance. In my mind, I said to myself "Not fancy, but clean." Oh, Lord, I sound more and more like my Mother! And then the trouble started. As Ed searched the room, there it was: "The Bathroom." All I had to do was to look at his face and I knew that all hell was going to break loose. The bathroom was a hole in the wall with a sink, a toilet and a God Damn bathtub! Our nightmare was coming true AGAIN! As Ed and I took a quick look at each other, he took on his detective role, opening up every door or closet which was in the room, but to no satisfaction. While I spoke to him calmly, saying "This can't be the room" , he was wheeling me out the door pushing me to God knows where. The front desk clerk knew immediately he was in deep shit as Ed asked him very rudely "Where in the hell is the so called "handicapped" room that was booked???" The guy, who had to be the desk clerk, had this look of complete puzzlement all over his face, saying "I have never been in the room, but it is a handicapped accessible room." Then Ed and I looked at each other wondering if we weren't crazy. In the meantime, the clerk walked in the back room, returning with a couple of keys on this chain. The keys to this imaginary bathroom! We were guided in the direction of our room once more by a young man who worked at the inn with this mystery chain of keys in his hand. As he looked all over the room, he began to realize he had a task ahead of him because there were three different doors in this room and where each went to nobody knew.

Similar to what Ed did, he tried to open up each door by the knob but to no avail. Then the keys came out! What door did they go to? When the young man unsuccessfully tried one key after another to unlock the most obvious door that might lead into a bathroom, the three of us just seemed even more bewildered than before. Each of them would not fit into the lock or turn either clockwise or counter clockwise. All I knew was that I really had to go to the bathroom in the worst way and thought to myself, "There is going to be a wet spot on the rug if this so-called bathroom didn't exist!" It reminded me of this silly saying which my Nana Campbell used to repeat when I was growing up but that I never quite understood: "How dry I am, how wet I'll be, if I don't find the bathroom key." I guess throughout the centuries they used to lock bathrooms so the public could not just use them. Now I knew EXACTLY what it meant as I did a dance in my wheelchair and squeezing my cheeks together! While I was trying not to think running water of any sorts, I heard a door opening up. I prayed it was "The Bathroom" that I needed so badly. As Ed crossed the threshold and fumbled for the light switch, I could feel my heart racing. Then a big scream came from Ed "The bathroom is like a dance floor, Gail! Even the shower has no lip on it to step over." Meanwhile the young man who worked at the inn was just standing there totally dumbfounded as to what we were excited for. Of course, it was only a bathroom to him with a toilet, sink and shower. To me, it was a room with no limitations. I could take a shower without any worries about Ed or myself falling because of a minor little elimination of a lip on the front of the shower entrance, or a sink low enough to brush my teeth in. At this point I was in heaven….

This reminds me of another place we frequently go to almost every Christmas time to see the holiday lights or to celebrate a special occasion. The Nine Zero Hotel is an upper class hotel on Tremont Street almost across from Boston Common. The first time I went there was a couple of years ago, just to get away for a few days from my hectic life. Well, even there they did not have any idea what a wheel-in shower was. First they brought me up to rooms on the ninth and eighth floors, but there were tubs in both. Then I explained once more what I needed. "Oh!" I remembering them saying. Then down to the fourth floor we went. There it was! A "wheel-in" shower. What a bathroom this was, with Italian tile everywhere one looked and A WHEEL-IN SHOWER to boot!

Then there are two inns that are down in Provincetown, Massachusetts which I have to recommend highly. One is the Brass Key Inn located on Bradford Street, which is fully handicapped accessible with one totally equipped room with a wheel-in bathroom and shower. This room looks out upon a very nice pool adjoined by lush terraces of professionally manicured grounds of greenery and floral boxes. The compound of Victorian buildings is set up so that each room has its own view of the gardens. Along with these assets, the Brass Key has charm and a kind of warmth to its décor, with gold framed pictures of fishermen and fireplaces and/or tubs in numerous rooms to keep guests warm since it is open year round. Lastly, I want it to be known how wonderful and helpful the staff is to its guests.

The second is The Crown & Anchor Inn situated right on Commercial Street. It is handicapped accessible and has its own restaurant, piano bar and cabaret club.

Back to Maine - as soon as "the bathroom" scene was over, Ed unpacked our clothes and we spent the rest of the afternoon on our deck overlooking downtown Boothbay Harbor and playing Scrabble with a couple of cocktails in front of us.

The next day we decided to attempt going downtown once more despite last year's disaster. Instead of getting in the car and going through the trouble of locking my wheelchair in the van, we walked, or rather Ed walked and I wheeled over the famous Boothbay Harbor footbridge into town. This time we went with a positive attitude. There ware not going to be any such things as architectural obstacles or barriers confronting us on this beautiful, sunny, magnificent day. What a joke that was! Right away I was going down a steep hill with Ed saying "I won't let you go, Gail, but my feet are slipping!" Instantly I put my right foot down trying to stop my wheelchair, but to no avail. I was going down and all I remembered was my mother's face the day I tipped over in our driveway into the gutter drain on Vine Street while she was looking at something in the backyard, failing to remember to put my brakes on. That memory will always be there until I die! I could even imagine her voice on the phone if I had fallen, starting out with "Oh, my God!" Well, as you know by now I survived the hill without a side trip to St. Andrews Hospital, although I looked at Ed throughout the day with complete disbelief at the danger he placed us both in.

After we ate lunch, which was only a takeout salad for Ed and a Reuben sandwich for me that was not worth the terrifying journey at all, we started going around the town discovering new ways to get around the different stores and quaint shops. There were sales everywhere, so I did a little Christmas shopping and got a Boothbay Harbor sweatshirt for myself. Like I really needed another top! As Ed wheeled me up and down curb after curb, I just wondered to myself whether society would ever understand or comprehend what obstacles I have to go through each day and hour of my life. Just going shopping or getting a bite to eat in this bustling, quaint town of Boothbay Harbor was a big task in and of itself. It was like a maze in a way and if one takes a curb the wrong way, one goes back to the beginning to start over again. Or the worst case scenario would be tipping over in one's wheelchair, hitting one's head on the hard concrete pavement while other tourists either just stroll by giving strange looks or completely ignoring the whole scene like I was an invisible piece of road kill, thinking to themselves, "She belongs in an institution. How come she's out in public, anyway?" If only a fraction of these strangers, and surprisingly some of my relatives, ever knew or truly took the time and effort to listen to me they would hide their faces in shame. On top of it all, if they realized that they, themselves, could become disabled to some degree in the next five minutes, what would they do or feel and how would they react? It would all become a different ballgame because it would be happening to them: the strange looks or stares, the fast glances ,or the gawking as if I had two heads that I so often take notice of .

After a couple hours of shopping and window browsing, I had had enough so back to the motel we went. On our way back we discussed whether to go on a sightseeing boat tour the next day, which was Wednesday. The focus of our discussion was whether the boat would be "handicapped accessible." This inquiry is always going to be the first consideration I need to ask whenever and wherever I go until they put me in the ground. At that point the question would be , "How are the undertakers at Rocco & Sons Funeral Home in Everett going to lie me straight in my casket with my legs being so atrophied due to not walking since I was ten?" On this cheerful reflection, we started our investigation on the different tour boats. Surprisingly the search took only five minutes .By just walking over to where they dock the boats and asking that dreaded question: "Are the tour boats wheelchair accessible?" Sometimes I think the question of accessibility should have been tattooed on my forehead when I was born because it would have saved me a lot of time, sweat and aggravation.

We headed toward town by foot the next day at around 11:30. I had a piece of pizza to eat knowing buying anything on the boat would be double priced and very limited. When I finished, we only had to go a short distance to Pier One to meet the woman at the customer's booth to find out what boat we were going on and informing her that I might need a hand getting on and off of the ferry with the wheelchair. And, thank goodness that I did! As a man escorted us up onto the pier, I noticed that there was this 90° angled gangplank staring us in the face head on. I looked at him without wavering and asked, "Have you ever done this before?" He laughed with a smile on his face and said, "Of course, lady." I honestly do not recall how the man brought me up the steep gangway, front ways or backwards, but it was a scary feeling to have some stranger in complete control of my safety and indeed my very life. Once aboard the Cap'n Combo which was owned by the Cap'n Fish's Boat Tours, I was relieved for two minutes until I started to feel the motion of the waves. I looked at Ed right away and he knew by the look on my face that I was starting to feeling sick. Automatically, he diverted my attention by starting up a conversation with me while I practiced the lessons the cruises' staff taught me over the years. As I looked at the horizon where the sky meets the ocean, the sick feeling dissipated. It worked, and fortunately this day the sea was so very calm. I truly think a lot of these types of situations are psychologically induced. Prior to our departure, Ed took me to a table where we could take in the whole tour, starting from Pier One throughout the Damariscotta and Pemaquid areas. As the tour guide was telling the passengers on the ship the history of the areas we were going through, many passengers remarked on the beautiful and huge homes which were built right on the waterfront. I know that by the end of this two hour excursion, all of us had our dream home in our minds forever. It seemed money had no limit in these areas. It seemed to be plentiful here, yet why not in other areas of Maine? As I soon learned, several homes had been built years back by businessmen who own big corporations. I guess the saying "Money comes to money!" is true. As soon as we got out far enough there were islands after islands, one with a famous lighthouse on it, some with two to three houses, likely with no electricity, plumbing, or connection to the outside chaotic world, some inhabited by seals who survive by eating other animals in the sea. It was funny just to view them doing the same antics over and over in a five minute period. Imagine doing that day after day. What tiny brains they must have!

Before Ed and I knew it, the boat was being docked back at the pier. While all of the passengers were sayings their goodbyes and best wishes to each other, I was swept away by the guide to go down the gangplank backwards. Maybe this was better because I could not see what was behind me. Of course, it was then snack time again. As with any vacation, food, sleep and shopping were the primary concerns . So onward the two of us went in search for a nearby, accessible restaurant. We gave our business to the first one we found. It was nothing fancy at all but it was located right on the waterfront and wheelchair friendly. Once inside, right away the atmosphere did not impress me. The dining room had a smell of mold which turned my stomach. I was and am very delicate when it comes to food or cleanliness. I guess I can blame my mother for this attribute, because ever since I can remember she was always cleaning or wiping something down. I was extremely grateful when the hostess asked us if we wanted to eat inside or out on the deck.

While Ed pushed my chair toward the patio, we had to go in through the dining room and bar area, and how glad I was that we were going to eat outside. The whole establishment smelled strongly of mildew and booze from the bar. Thankfully I was headed for the fresh sea air. While we were contemplating what to order, the waitress brought us our drinks, a margarita for me and a beer for Ed, which were pretty good. Who could screw up a margarita or a beer? What am I talking about: China of the Sea Restaurant did exactly that last year! Anyway, the food was not top-notch. I did not like what I ordered. It was shrimp in a Cancun sauce with green and red peppers. It sure did not satisfy my taste buds. Of course, when I ordered it from the menu, the waitress said "Good choice." She was wrong as I left three thirds of the appetizer uneaten. My Dad's voice echoed through my head, "Kids over in Korea are starving eating out of the garbage." He brought this saying to his grave as I will bring it to mine.

Soon we were back at the hotel. It was Wednesday night and the next day we planned to go to Freeport, which everyone called the "Town of Outlets." How true this was. There were outlets and discount stores all around town that sold shoes, hats and everything in-between. Ed went for the shoes. I went in between for the purses and the pants. We had a ball.

It was like being in candy land for a child. The one thing which was an obstacle was the jewelry story, Zale's, with no way for me to get in. Maybe it was a blessing, but just to know that I could not get in made me angry. This was discrimination at its best but, again, this was and IS part of my world of not being able to walk up or down stairs. As I sat in my wheelchair overlooking the store from afar, I only could laugh thinking in my mind "If they ever saw the jewelry I have just on my body!" Oh, well.....

After Ed went on his personal excursions, I was so hungry since I'd skipped breakfast. As the reader by now knows, this was quite a task. I was wheeled up and down curbs and sidewalks, looking for an impossible to find wheelchair accessible restaurant. But finally we found or thought we found one. Ed, being a very stubborn and determined man, saw this place across the street on Main, on a very hilly incline, and so, of course, as all little boys do , Ed had to investigate the crime scene. The name of the place was called Azure Italian Café. At first glance, it seemed to be inaccessible with different levels and landings but after Ed inquired about whether they had accessibility for a wheelchair, the staff was extremely helpful. A gentleman, who at the time we did not know was the owner, escorted us to an outside patio table. So, as usual, Ed ordered drinks and then we peaked at the luncheon menu. Every appetizer and entrée sounded so mouth-watering and unique that it took me a couple of minutes to decide what to finally order. Finally the decisions were made with painstaking care. I requested the Maine Seafood Cakes consisting of crab, salmon, shrimp and scallops served with a spicy carrot and parsnip ribbons. I was a little apprehensive about this appetizer, hoping that it did not have an overwhelming fishy taste, but as I took my first mouthful it was amazing. As far as Ed's food was concerned, he only had lasagna. I grew up with macaroni dishes all of my life so lasagna was lasagna. I changed my entire perspective on lasagna on this day though. It was not heavy like I remembered it to be. It was so light with four different layers of four kinds of cheeses in it. I had a taste of it before Ed devoured it all. It was simply delicious and delightful. I would say we overstayed our welcome because all of a sudden our waitress was nowhere to be seen and a gentleman walked up to our table , which was the only occupied table in the whole restaurant, inquiring on how we were doing. Ed said to the man ,"The food was so good!" as I nodded my head in mutual agreement. Little did we know he was the owner of Azure until we got into a deep conversation about Ed and I not being from around the state of Maine but having vacationed there over the two past summers.

The conversation went on for several minutes like he knew us for years. We found out he and his wife opened up the restaurant a couple years ago and, although he loves it, it takes a lot of time away from his family. Prior to us leaving and indulging in more eating, I said to the owner that I was in the process of writing an autobiography and that it was so difficult to travel in a wheelchair 95% of the time and that I was going to put in a recommendation for his restaurant. He was smiling from ear to ear as Ed and I said our goodbyes and best wishes for the years to come.

On our way back to our motel, we picked up our already purchased merchandise, sometimes parking in the middle of the street so a staff member could put whatever into my car.

That evening, just to relax and hang low, we ate at the inn's restaurant. I only had lobster bisque which was just all right and nothing to rave about. Just sitting there talking and waiting for our check to come, all of a sudden the waitress came to our table wishing us a "Good Night." But, she had no check in her hand. When she came by again, we asked her "Could we have our check?" and in response she said "Somebody picked up your check!" Of course, I said "No, no, no! Who paid for our meal?" Of course, we did not get any-where and walked gingerly back to our room.

The next two days we celebrated our eleven years of friendship and visited Doug and Christine on our way back home.

Chapter 10

Fun In The Sun

I went for a week to Bermuda for the third time with my soul mate in September of 1996 on the Royal Majesty Cruise Line. It was my first cruise so I did not know what to expect. Let me tell you, it was another adventure which I will never forget. The room was so small that I had a bad case of claustrophobia. On top of this, there were only two small portholes that served as windows to look out from. They were too high up for me to see out of in my wheelchair. The worst of it: "The Bathroom!" It was a hole in the wall that even walking people would have had a hard time getting in and out of, not to mention an individual who had to be carried and helped in by another person. The only good thing about it was that the bathroom was all tiled so I took my daily shower while sitting on the toilet.

Dinner time was another adventure. Each passenger was assigned a table for the week and this was another obstacle to contend with. The people we were assigned to sit with simply avoided any type of conversation and eye contact. It was like we weren't there. So, what is new! All week, Ed and I were simply disregarded at the dinner table. It was as though we were invisible. I truly feel that in the back of their minds they were thinking that this was never going to happen to them, but then again one never knows what is in one's deck of cards.

When we docked in Bermuda, we took off by ourselves to sightsee and explore. There was even a taxi for the disabled so we hired the driver, named Roderick (all of the locals called him "Colonel") , for a day to take us all over the island. We were taken all through downtown Hamilton, touring churches and art galleries, while the afternoon was designated for the beach. This was my favorite spot, where I sat in my wheelchair overlooking the clear, aqua marine ocean in the scanty white bathing suit which I purposely purchased for this trip. I noticed this tree to my right bending over with the wind. It looked like the tree that I had painted years ago for Joel.

Everything was so perfect until we realized we were not alone. Some fellow passengers came to enjoy the serenity and tranquility of the area too. On the way back to the ship I saw the unique pastel colors of homes and buildings where the natives lived or worked.

I also noticed how they treated their infirmed population in that society. It was similar to cultures all over Europe. They warehoused them up on a hill where they were out of sight and mind. I guess this was why the average person on the island or the cruise ship stared at, ignored, or admired us both. Whatever they believed, Ed and I broke every previous notion they had.

I've been to Aruba twice in the last ten years. We stayed at the Aruba Marriott Resort both times. The Island of Aruba is generally very friendly and safe, despite what went on last April or May involving an American high school graduate. The people who live there highly depend on tourists for their salary so any upset would impact their lives.

The weather is just perfect with always a slight, warm wind ruffling through the trees all over the island.

We always stay on the sixth or seventh floor, because there are a few so called disabled rooms that have bigger bathrooms. I recall this was not the case on one trip where they directed us into this room on the second floor with a tree growing in front of our window, blocking our view of the beautiful scenery. I automatically indicated that I never booked this room. Instead I told the bell hop, "This is a mistake, because I would never book a room that did not over look the ocean in any way, shape or form." I guess they realized I meant business, because in fifteen minutes we were brought up to a nice room on the sixth floors which included a sitting room, a view anyone would die for, and a wheel out balcony.

Sometimes it pays to have a big mouth!

On one trip to Aruba Ed and I wanted to go on a dinner/booze cruise. Upon our arrival at the dock I looked at the gangplank and saw that the gangplank was too narrow to accommodate the wheels on my wheelchair. After arguing with Ed for five minutes, telling him point blank that this was an impossible task to perform, out of nowhere two burly crew members lifted me (wheelchair and all) above their heads. I became scared shitless as I was floating in mid air thirty feet above the water, just praying that they would not drop me. It is a good thing this was a BOOZE cruise, because boy did I need a drink!!!

Las Vegas was another learning experience for Ed and me. I am glad that I went but I shall never go back again. The daily average temperature was 100 degrees or more of dry heat and the primary activity was gambling. All you can see are hotel after hotel to gamble away your money.

First, I am not a so-called "gambler." If I bet fifty dollars on Blackjack, that would be it for the night.

I had two quite comical incidents in Las Vegas. While at the crowded pool Ed went to get a lounge chair for himself but in the meantime he forgot to put on my wheelchair brakes. Well, as I felt my chair moving towards the pool I panicked, placing my good right foot down on the ground trying to stop myself from rolling into it. I managed to get the chair stopped just in time.

The second happened when we were departing our hotel for the airport to get the plane back to Boston. Ed and I had made previous arrangements days before for a handicapped equipped taxi to pick us up at the hotel but to our dismay the cab never came, so I needed to get lifted out of my wheelchair in an ordinary passenger taxi without any safety straps or seat belt. By the time I arrived at the airport I was on the floor of the cab. The look on the driver's face was of disbelief. He thought that I was drunk. This is the impression that I have given in many everyday events but this was one which strikes me as being one of a kind. I do have to say that during about ninety-five percent of my travels I always had to confront society's stereotype about people with disabilities.

One of my unique tales was when I traveled on an airplane. Just the ordeal of simply getting aboard to my assigned seat starts my vacations off badly. I tell them how I am not able to walk but they still ask, "Can you walk at all?" In the meantime, Ed already is getting more and more irritated saying "No, she can't stand up at all! She has to be lifted." The individuals in charge of handicapped affairs just stood by my wheelchair with a look of complete bewilderment all over their faces, without a clue about what to do next. Finally, they got an aisle seat for me but when I was lifted into it I discovered there were no seat belts attached to the chair. Of course, with me having Cerebral Palsy this was a disaster just waiting to happen because I do not have sense any of balance. As Ed cried out "Gail needs to be strapped in!" I just recalled in the middle of this chaos, one of the men suggested removing his pants belt to tie me on to the small aisle chair until I got to my plane seat. This made Ed furious and he ordered this man to go to find another aisle chair with the right equipment on it!

Another example is when I went out to have lunch at a Chinese restaurant called Fantasy Island in Swampscott, Massachusetts. When I order a drink the waiter outright refuses saying to get me one, saying "You already had too many." My Ed walks with a limp, therefore the waiter branded him as a drunk too. Ed promptly stood up and talked to the manager to complain and we left the establishment never to return again. I can only say that there is so much ignorance out in the world, but I am hoping to teach every person who reads this book not to judge by appearance alone.

I went out to dine at The Continental Restaurant in Saugus with my Personal Care Attendant, Joy. Ed had gone to Colorado for the weekend with his Dad and a couple of uncles to a Patriot's football game. Joy stayed over and we had a ball that Saturday night. There was a short, funny looking, white haired man walking to our table and he proceeded to serve us as if he was applying for a job at Windsor Castle. He was so formal and he refused to crack a smile. His name was Bobby. Joy asked him what he was doing with a bowl around his neck and he told her it was once used for wine tasting. In the meantime, Joy and I had one eye on the door anticipating the arrival of someone I had a score to settle with. The lounge was packed and so was the bar. The appetizers that were brought to our table over the course of an hour were delicious and varied. We had bean dip, popovers and chicken wings to eat with our wine. The approximate age of the crowd, except for Joy and I, was sixty to seventy. We put our dinner order in and ordered another bottle of wine as the band started. The next thing we knew in came old man Bobby marching towards our table like a gunslinger in the old west ready for a fight. A fight he got! After he told us, while looking at me, that we could not get another bottle of wine I felt my anger rise because I have been through this many times before. Joy was not happy with this little prick's attitude either. Calmly, she asked why and he told us that he had been working as a wine server, (which he gave us a fancy word for) at The Continental for thirty-five years so HE ought to know the rules. He did not get away with his act and when Joy asked him what his problem was he said we had to order our main course first, which we had already done and she told him so. A woman seated at the table beside us overheard the whole thing and told us that the way he spoke to us was totally out of line. When he returned with our wine, he opened it and slammed into the ice bucket without adding ice. Joy was a restaurant manager and she knew this kind of treatment was unacceptable. She went to get the manager and told him what happened. He immediately found Bobby and spoke with him and then he came to our table to let us know it was all taken care of. It was obvious that we had succeeded in pushing Bobby off his high horse because he could not look at us for the rest of the night. From then on, each time we go to The Continental Restaurant, we are treated like paying customers with dignity and respect. I even received this letter:

dear gail

> *we received your letter recently and we apologize for the way bob acted. i have spoken to bob personally and i can assure you, this situation will never happen to any of our customers again. i am asking you that the next time you dine in the continental, please ask for me*

thank you
athas kourkoulis
president

In 2001 I began a new lifestyle: nudism. It is not at all like it sounds. Most people first hearing this automatically thinks of sex and orgies, but it was not like this with my soul mate and I.

Our first vacation as nudists was at Cypress Cove Resort in Kissimmee, Florida. As we drove our rental car up to the gated entrance, an attendant asked for our reservation name. In return, we got a sticker for the car window. While we drove to the main office, we saw trailers and campers. As Ed went into the office to pay for our room I suddenly saw naked people walking, riding bicycles, motor scooters and golf carts. At that moment,

I thought to myself, "What the hell are we doing here?!" When Ed came back, I tried to get the look of surprise off my face. Getting into our room was a shear relief to me. As we undressed to go out into this strange environment I could feel the sweat coming down from my armpits. No, my deodorant did not work that day!

As our villa door closed, the both of us were naked outside. Here we went into uncharted territory as we headed to the bar "Cheeks" to get a drink. Two stiff drinks! We quickly worked our way to the bar and ordered two drinks. In the meantime, everyone else was just having fun, talking or laughing. To our surprise, everyone was friendly and not looking at our naked bodies. I was not even gazed at for being in a wheelchair. In this new environment I realized I was not a threat to society anymore. I was equal instead of being an outcast on the other side of the fence.

In the first couple of years on vacations at Cypress Cove, Ed and I have met quite a variety of individuals who either turned out to be best friends or complete idiots just like in the "real" world. There was Trish and Neil, who looked to be educated, married, and met us in our early years at the resort when we wanted to experience being naked in the hot tub. As Ed and I wondered how in the hell we would accomplish this task with my whole body being dysfunctional in every way possible and with Ed's right side affected with a slight case of WONDERFUL Cerebral Palsy, Trish and Neil came right away to our rescue. All they asked was "How can we help?" It helped with finding out later that Trish was a nurse and from then on we have been friends since, despite the long distance between us outside of the resort.

Then there's the trailer trash that live in Cypress Cove. Usually, one partner goes out into the big, cruel, competitive world that starts right outside the gated entrance of the cove and the other does odd jobs for the resort, getting paid only for those jobs and borrowing money from their partner for beer, thus putting aside food or real nourishment for their bodies, minds and souls.

Three years after our first trip, Ed, Julie (who was working for me as a Personal Care Attendant then) and I went again and I experienced my first disappointment in Julie and Cypress Cove. Ed wanted the night off from worrying about taking care of me so I informed Julie that she was officially on duty that night. Yes, right! As she was downing mudslides, I could see she was getting loaded by the half hour and all of a sudden she was nowhere to be seen. We found her back in her room fast asleep. As Ed put me in bed, my body bounced up off the mattress and my nose happened to hit Ed's forehead. Oh, the PAIN! I had a black eye for days.

We experienced our first Florida hurricane in Cypress Cove on this trip, too. When the lights went out so did the water for our toilet and the electricity. The entire staff working at the resort disappeared as well. Ed solved the toilet situation by going bare assed down to this new duck pond right outside our room and filled up buckets of water to flush the toilet each time we went to the bathroom. We had to cope with the rest of this bad and quite serious situation without food or contact with the outside world until Monday morning. The few guests that were there included two couples from England, who offered us some supper from their tiny outdoor grill. For the rest of the weekend we ate junk food that was given to Ed and I days earlier at a timeshare purchase. As for our drinking needs, we had only wine, beer and Sambuca.

When Monday morning rolled around, the owner and staff tried their hardest to make up for their lack of responsibility and gave everyone a free breakfast. At the same time, the resort actually expected us to pay ground fees for those two days. Oh boy, did they receive a nasty letter from me in days to come!

So, until this book gets published, this has been our lifestyle during the past five years without relatives or friends knowledge, except for my mom. The facts came to her a couple of years ago when she was helping me unpack after one of my excursions at Cypress Cove. As she unpacked my one suitcase, asking me what was clean or dirty; the clean clothes pile was overflowing on my bed. A baffled look loomed across my mother's face as to say, "What did you wear during your week's vacation?" This was when I began the laughter which was pent up inside of me. I had to tell her the truth, the whole truth. I simply said, "I'm a nudist, Ma." While I repeated it several times in different sentence forms, suddenly she yelled "Nudist?!" As I nodded my head up and down, I can still hear her warning: "Do not EVER "say" this to anybody in the family!" I guess I did not keep my promise, because I'm writing it down.

We have been to Paradise Lakes near Tampa, which is mainly for swingers. We honestly thought about swinging during prior years, but it never materialized, thank God. As years traveled passed Ed and I have been on nudist cruises to St. Marten, St. Lucia, St. Thomas, Nassau, Dominican Republic and Catalina Island

As the decades go by, I know that the world will slowly change its attitude towards the disabled in general. The reactions, the attitudes, and the looks which I continuously come across over and over are parallel. Either I am totally ignored or treated like I have two heads, EVEN at my favorite vacation spot or on cruises. This is my life until my passing, so I need to come to the knowledge that people are just people and change is almost impossible until it touches their lives in some way or time.

In the future we will be going on a reunion nudist cruise to Key West, Jamaica and on to Mexico. The next year we are scheduled for a cruise to Hawaii.

CHAPTER 11

ADVENTURES THEN AND NOW

In the late 1960's my first camp experience was at Camp Jollee which was near Spring-field, Massachusetts. I despised this whole experience immensely. The hatred started with the three hour ride to the western part of Massachusetts in the middle of a July heat wave. From here on everything continued downhill because it reminded me so much of Crotched Mountain with similar restrictions and rules. Also, I was taken away from my family once more. Every minute of the three week session was timed. As I went forward in life I came to the knowledge that this rigid timing business would be a big thing in my world.

I attended Camp Sea Haven when I was around seventeen. Sea Haven was located overlooking the frigid ocean in Plum Island, Massachusetts. It was first started after World War II when an epidemic of Polio geared the community towards recreation and therapeutic programs for children. After the Salk Vaccine to prevent Polio was developed, the camp was turned into a recreational camp for children and adults with Cerebral Palsy, with 250 individuals attending each summer until it closed in 1987.

I was one of the older campers at Camp Sea Haven then, so I just laughed my way through it. I realized how to play along with the rules better. I met many young counselors three to five years younger than myself. I never quite figured out why some were working there. The pay was terrible and the hours long and living conditions just barely tolerable. All I can say is that each had a personality or weirdness of his/her own, surely making camp life more interesting. There were the male and female counselors who were all different from one another: straight, gay, and the bi, and the loose ones. As long as their lifestyles did not affect me I did not care, but it did affect me in time. One of the loose ones was Iris. How could I have known that she would have an everlasting impact on my ignorance of life? Iris was a Jewish, free spirited individual. This is a gentle term to describe her now. In time, I heard stories about her escapades. One of them was when a group of people went to Squam Lake in New Hampshire and she

Beyond The Wheelchair

took off her top while she swam. She was very fortunate I was not there, because I would have given her a piece of my mind. She literally thought sex was the way to get a man. I guess she learned the hard way that this type of behavior did not attract the right man because years later I heard her husband was a wife abuser.

Then there was Robb who became a friend. He was only approaching fourteen years old when he first started working at the camp. At first I wondered why he ever wanted to work with the disabled but in years to come I knew why. Like us, he wanted to be accepted. In later years, I found out that Robb was gay like I always suspected but never wanted to admit. Life was hard enough living the straight life, not to mention the prejudices which went along with a gay lifestyle. We supported each other when life dealt us a bad set of cards until he moved out west to San Francisco to live his lifestyle as a homosexual individual without judgment and ridicule. Although I knew inside of me that he was gay, the reality of him moving so far away and his lifestyle, which I do not believe I will ever fully accept, was harsh at that time. It was actually pushed in my face in a letter I received just prior to New Year's of 1978. The news came forcefully on me as I read his sarcastic words on pieces of note paper. It was like a joke Robb was springing on me. For years I struggled with this truth when attending the gay bars and restaurants where he worked as a bookkeeper. His flirtations toward other men and his outward affections to other males bothered me. I don't even like to see heterosexual couples all over each other as I always professed to him. My opinion is there is a place and time for everything.

The final straw came when I contacted Doug three years ago and Robb said, "After all he did to you, Gail?" Robb hasn't even talked to me since.

Camp Sea Haven was like any other camp. The beds were just cots with one thin, uncomfortable mattress on each of them. The food mainly consisted of cold cereal or lumpy oatmeal in the morning. So delicious! Each small, cramped, wooden cabin, which was segregated by gender surrounded a platform where a flag pole stood. Each held three to four campers, depending on how severe their disability was, and one or two camp counselors. It was like being in the Army or Crotched Mountain again. Instead of waking up by a switch of bright, glaring dorm florescent lights at five o'clock in the morning, we were forced to hear this annoying,

135

out of tune bugle at seven or seven thirty. How I hated that bugle! I thought camp was supposed to be fun, like a vacation. But let me tell you, this was no vacation. As usual, every waking hour was scheduled. We were greeted in the mornings by either a Kellogg's small cold cereal, oatmeal or, on rare occasion, pancakes which could be used as Frisbees. After breakfast came clean up which consisted of making the cots and straightening up the cabin. About nine o'clock the official day began with good old camp activities such as arts & crafts, archery, painting and so forth. All the counselors who were hired had no former experience with or knowledge of working with the disabled so they had their hands full with teaching teenagers from the ages of fourteen to eighteen years old. How fun was this? Many of the male counselors did not know what they were doing so they faked it. Their minds were at the beach or pool where they could be in the sun, making believe they were working and entertaining us. The pool was hardly in use and always in need of repair, or so I was told, but I actually think it was just an excuse to get some sun. Soon noon came along with apprehension as to what would be facing us called food. It was like a crap shoot. Food was placed in front of you and you either ate or starved. Many of us took the easy way out by eating peanut butter and jelly sandwiches. At least we knew we would be safe, whichever method we chose. At one o'clock sharp it was rest period. No matter how hard I tried I could not get out of it. The hour seemed like three. How could we be tired? We did not do much of anything in the morning. The afternoons were for swim time. With no workable pool three fourths of the time we went down to the beach through sand dunes and grassy areas. It was like an amusement park ride getting down to the beach if you were in a wheelchair and where one's stomach landed, nobody knew! Little did I know that the beach was a nightly hide away for many counselors? God only knows what went on in the dark of the night.

Then one summer there was a tall, handsome, all American counselor who only worked at camp for a year or two who has had quite an influence on me to this very day. This was the first time I fell in love. There were many male counselors over the years, but this one was different. Doug was educated, handsome and witty. I first met him around 1972 while he was working at Camp Sea Haven. He had sandy, blonde, thick wavy hair and a knock out smile. I knew him for about four and a half years. We never dated but we went out on trips with the Cerebral Palsy Boston Association to Bermuda or Cape Cod. I vividly recall going to Squam Lake up in

New Hampshire one weekend with two other friends, my cousin Kathy, and him. When we arrived at his parents' cabin it was around dusk in the middle of nowhere. It was a log cabin with a wooden stove and two bunk beds. Being a city girl and going to my grandparents' rental cottages or my parents' house on the Cape during all of my childhood from the day of my conception, I was scared to death. I was way out of my comfort zone, especially when I found out there was no bathroom but an outhouse instead. Thank goodness I brought my bed pan because there was no chance in hell I was going out in complete darkness to go to the bathroom! That evening was full of laughter and ghosts stories. "The Green Hand" was one of his creations, which at the time and place had me scared to the point that I wanted to kill him. Of course, I had no idea that Douglas Preston would become a famous writer in years to come!

He broke my heart when we both took a ride to camp one day in the summer of 1976 and decided to stay that night. We had got back to camp later than we realized after a night out on the town. There were four or five of us who slept on the beach. It was a beautiful, starlit night with the gentle sound of the waves to lull us to sleep. When all got settled, I was still awake for some time due to a back brace I had to wear after the two operations I had in 1975. As I lay there, all of a sudden I heard two people moving on my left. It was Iris and Doug kissing. How I just wanted to die. Something in me did die that night. A huge piece of me died which would be dead forever; a piece of my heart and dignity. Everybody knew how I felt about him, except for him. It took me years to get him out of my mind and heart.

No, he never knew me . . . . .

Early morning as we drove home in complete silence, I could feel the tension in the air and I just could not look at him. The next time I saw him was at Robb's apartment for a Christmas get together. After a couple of drinks, we went in a quiet room to talk. Much earlier I had written to him about the event. Of course, he was in denial but it was what he said to me that simply shocked me. He talked to me as a cripple, not a friend. Neither love nor sex was a part of my life or existence, he said. Now as I look back, I see how foolish I acted for months after. I was not eating, sleeping and cried over everything. Finally, he became a bitter memory and I swore to myself I would never care for any man again. Oh, how naive I was. I saw him twenty-eight years later at one of his book signings with my soul mate, Ed.

In between schooling, I had the great advantage to travel with the Cerebral Palsy of Greater Boston which was started by Edith Schneider. Mrs. Schneider, with CP herself, was the pioneer for the advancement for other individuals, especially adults with Cerebral Palsy, to acknowledge that they could have a "real" life out in society.

Mrs. Schneider was an extremely inspiring woman for her time and encouraged a lot of us to go forward in life. Ever since I met her at the age of 12, she was a great motivator for me in my life. She wanted us in the real world, so she was continuing thinking of programs and activities for us to be involved with.

I will always reminisce every other Thursday night was Chorus Group which was held at this church where we sang our lungs out. Imagine a group of individuals with speech impairments singing! Maybe we woke up the dead a few of those Thursday evenings.

Then there were evenings at the well known Arthur Murray Dance Studio located in Boston where we actually took dancing lessons in our wheelchair.

The first trip for the GB group was organized by a man named Loring Myette. Loring became a very special individual in my life throughout the rest of my years of traveling abroad. He had dreams of adventure and conquests for all of us with Cerebral Palsy. I first met him when I started attending the Cape weekends. He was either working behind the scenes preparing our meals or dressing us or wiping our asses. Loring began this tradition by receiving donations from several Cod Cape businesses and organizations like the Elk's Club and Knights of Columbus chapters to pay for our hotel rooms and meals. He did this well with his everlasting, robust energy. As the years passed, I knew he needed us as much as we needed him. It was like we were filling a hole in his existence, a hole that could not ever be filled by other human beings.

We went to Cape Cod, Massachusetts and stayed at the Blue Waters Motel in West Yarmouth for our first trip. I was only twelve years old then but what a memorable weekend that became. There were no elevators anywhere in the motel so the male volunteers lifted us up and down stairs when we needed to go swimming or eat. This was the first time the Cerebral Palsy Association organized a trip, so no one can be blamed for the ill planning. This became a regular trip each year in the months of February or March until I turned 47. It was here where I met many volunteers who remained in my life for years to come. One of them was Ben, a tall, silent man who at the time was living in his own hell as a chronic alcoholic. I wondered to myself at the time why he was even there, volunteering for the disabled, but, like Loring, they both were in need of a second chance to fill a gap in their lives. As the years rolled on, I saw this loneness which surrounded Loring but then I never realized he was living in a world which did not accept him either. He was gay, but never flaunted it or spoke about his personal life in front of us ever.

We stayed at different hotels around the Cape area. In the townships of Falmouth, Eastham and Hyannis there were places which donated their rooms for us to stay in and there were food and dining areas allotted to the Cape Cod Cerebral Palsy Winter Weekend (CCPW). These three days were always fun. All we did was eat, swim and party. Of course, the partying started when I was 21 years old! As far as the volunteers, they each had their own reasons to attend these getaways. Quite a lot of them came just to help or to do a good deed, but about eighty percent had a hand in it for their own selfish reasons: to party. And oh how well a few did this! One of them was Vicky who, of course, was assigned to me on one trip to the Sheraton in Eastham. As Saturday night ticked its way around, so did Vicky. She just sat in one place for hours, drinking her way to no man's land, crying the whole time. It was sad but what about her responsibility to me? There wasn't any as I finally found out when I needed to go to the bathroom and bed at one or two in the morning. Vicky was totally wasted by this time, so I had to ask another volunteer's help with the toilet and putting me to bed.

Then after twenty or so minutes I heard the hotel room door open, knowing it was Vicky by her unsteady steps and the slamming of the door. As she finally pissed and staggered into her bed, I thought this night was over, but it was not. About fifteen minutes later a knock on the door awoke me abruptly. As usual, because of my CP I jumped due to any fast or sudden noise. I could not believe what happened next. Vicky, as intoxicated as she was, stood up and opened the door. In the twilight of the dark room, I heard a man's voice as he followed Vicky to the bed. As I tried so hard to keep still and silent, the man's voice echoed throughout the room, although he was murmuring very softly. All I knew was that he was black and wanted something from Vicky like every man did. As he sat on the edge of her bed, I could only hear the silence of the night with a couple of moaning sounds coming from her. Then he disappeared, walking out as fast as he came in, never to be seen again.

These trips came to a stop, because donations declined.

Our huge yearly trips were scheduled for each fall, too. My first trip was to Florida in September 1967 when I fourteen. The reason I remember this trip so well was because I got my first period a few days prior. I knew I was leaving my childhood and growing up was in front of me. Lucky me, I guess! At that time, the modern conveniences such as walkways from the airport to the plane were not built yet, so we had to be literally lifted from the tarmac up the stairs of the plane. I still look back in wonderment at how the male volunteers did this amazing feat, especially when some of the passengers were dead weight , some weighing over two hundred pounds. Despite it all, the volunteers always did what they had to do without a complaint. They always wanted to be first in line to carry me, because I was the lightest. This became one of the main jokes. The second was over my left spastic arm which would not stay down by my side without a five pound arm weight on it. On one trip I injured one volunteer, Nuncio's, family jewels. As he walked passed my seat in the plane I hit him with my swinging arm. I do not think I will ever forget it and I laugh to myself every time I think about it. Nuncio was like a father figure to all of us. He always stood as the leader for all the volunteers. If one did not know him well he came off as domineering when he shouted out orders to other volunteers. However, he was a gentle giant. He was very efficient, which was needed for us to have smooth trips. As years continued to go by, I knew how much he cared about and loved us. But when I became an adult I began to realize he was cheating on his wife when going on trips with us which did not sit well with me. Maybe this was one of the reasons he drank so much?

In 1987, a small group of us went to Italy with an independent travel agent named Rocco. The first destination was Rome. Rome was a lot like I had pictured, with a lot of history and ruins, but I also saw another side of the city. The streets were dirty and our hotel turned out to be a whore house. Topping off the whole experience, there no way to get up to the bar. The elevator was so small that those in wheelchairs could not even fit in to get to their rooms. Plus the rooms looked like they had not been remodeled or painted for decades, with peeling wallpaper and faded walls. Even better was that the electricity was not up to code like here in America. One night when we were getting dressed to go out to dinner, the electricity went entirely out on our floor because of a blow dryer. It was the most depressing place I had ever been in, especially on a vacation. I did not even want to think who occupied the bed before me.

The most exhilarating memory I brought back with me from Rome was a session with Pope John Paul. He came up to me, his voice so gentle and calm and he said, "You come from Boston?" As I struggled to say "Yes" he just stood in front of me with such a tranquil and serene mood surrounding him, as if the thousands of other worshipers in the square did not exist. As he blessed me and my set of rosary beads which I purchased there, I could feel his gentle touch on my forehead making the sign of the cross. Those rosary beads I placed in my dad's hands when he passed away....

The next place we traveled was to the magnificent and mountainous city of Sorrento, Italy to this beautiful hotel overlooking the aqua blue Mediterranean Ocean and the Isle of Capri. Many took a boat over to Capri, but it was not accessible to a lot of us who were in wheelchairs. What else is new?!

The next adventure was a bus trip along the Amalfi Coast. As we passed other buses and cars our hearts were in our mouths because of the vertical cliffs that were directly to our left. Either one vehicle had to back up or drive forward for the other to pass. Aside from these death obstacles, it was simply breathtaking and gorgeous.

Our room was just as graceful, with Italian tiled floor and a patio which I took great advantage of after five o'clock in the evenings with a cocktail and a view out over the most peaceful place I have ever seen. When the sun went down one could see lights etching out the mountains and the landscapes of Sorrento and the Isle of Capri.

Everywhere I looked, as we ventured out some evenings for dinner along the cobblestone streets etched between stores, marketplaces and limestone apartments, I saw people either conversing, eating, playing cards or dancing. As I passed them in my wheelchair, I knew this is how it was meant to be. It was all about family and the human race, connecting with one another in good and bad times. This is how it was when I was growing up and neighbors came out of their houses and had a minute to say "Hi" or "How are you?" Now people are too busy keeping up with the Joneses or forging ahead full speed through life and getting locked up in their own worlds of self indulgence. So, I reveled in this fantasy for a few days.

After our nightly voyages, we slithered back to the hotel where a few of us went straight to the swimming pool. Some either went in clothed or striped down to their underwear. What fun we had behind Mr. Rocco's back. God only knew what he was doing after we found out he had propositioned every female volunteer on the trip.

Over the years, Loring planned several trips for part of the Cerebral Palsy Group. One of them was Switzerland. On this trip my cousin Anna Maria went with me. The other trip was with Ben, Sue, Roger, Roger's wife, etc. It was absolutely magnificent. I have never seen so many mountains and gorgeous terrain ever in my life. We mainly traveled by bus and train. We stayed up at Mt. Rigi the first night. Although at the time I did not know it was because of migraine headaches , I headed right to the lady's room at the airport to puke my guts out. I just wanted to die. Loring said the next day that I had literally turned green! All I recall was getting up to this hotel in the heavens and going to bed. I remember the next day was simply stunning and breathtaking. We were overlooking the clouds like we were in heaven. We were actually above the clouds looking down upon the earth. A feeling of immense peace came upon me that I never felt before.

It was on this trip that we traveled by bus to each destination. I will always remember the tour at a cheese factory in Switzerland. Well, let me tell you, as soon as we drove into this small town, we knew we were in cow land due to the stench of cow dung permeating through the air. The best is yet to come. After taking an excursion through the cheese factory, I was swept away by a volunteer, Ben, to venture outside, where he wheeled me up this hill to overlook the whole town. During this quest, I kept on smelling this appalling stench. As Ben and I reached the top of the hill, I looked down at the wheels of my chair and saw cow shit in my wheel spokes. By this time, we saw others wheeling up to see what we were up to. Little did they know what they were getting themselves into! After we took a couple of pictures of the group and the gorgeous mountainous terrain, we had to get to the bus that was down the hill. So once again, we braced ourselves to go down this hill full with cow dingle-berries and sat in this foul aroma all the way home to our hotel.

In the days to come, we traveled by train to the south of Switzerland and stayed in Lucerne which was a lively place and the most gorgeous city I ever saw. The architecture made Lucerne a magnificent and most out of the ordinary city . Each building and home was embellished with its own unique design and colors. This was a tour within itself. Nights we walked around Lucerne looking for excitement. This was hard because, as one knows, they start eating dinner at 8 pm and dinner lasts sometimes for over two and a half hours. On this particular trip the climate was freezing so the eight of us in our group were bundled up in layers of clothing. It was downright cold, penetrating right to the bone. One night Ben found this coffee shop/restaurant a couple of blocks from our hotel so we went there the remaining nights we had in Lucerne. A woman approximately in her late 50's or early 60's was the owner and was simply amazed at us. She never had the experience of seeing disabled individuals traveling, never mind out at midnight trying to get warm and have fun. She was so in awe of us that she and her family invited the group, about 40 of us, to dinner prior to leaving.

The next stop was to Lugano, Switzerland, right at the base of this beautiful country. It is the biggest city in Ticino and the main language spoken was Italian. I just recall there were mountains enveloping the entire city like a protective mother looking over her offspring so no harm would get to them. We ate a brief bite of lunch there of some sort of macaroni and after taking a couple of pictures we were on the train again.

As the train curved around tracks for hours on end, one could not help noticing the majestic beauty of Switzerland. There were snow capped mountains everywhere you looked. Once in awhile there appeared a valley with a couple of houses and a church. I was so curious about how these people lived or survived there? What did they do for work or leisure? They seemed to be so isolated from the world, but in another sense, so contented being away from the hustle of life.

Although the scenery was so overpowering, I was getting sick of sitting in one position in my wheelchair. This is so true, especially when I'm in a plane seat where I can't reposition myself due to the angle of the seat and being restricted by a seat belt. I call to mind that this anguish went away when Ben picked me up and opened up the train window to give me a view of the mountains passing by.

Another trip was to Munich, Germany and on to England where we toured castles and homes of Winston Churchill. How manicured they were and how stately they stood with acres and areas of the most manicured lawns I ever seen. In the days to come, we traveled up to Edinburgh, Scotland where there were pastures of green everywhere. There was the color of green as far and wide as the eye could see. As we passed through small town-ships, life seemed to be so at ease. The contrast between America and Scotland was glaringly apparent. People were not in a hurry. I guess this applies to all of Europe.

Once in Scotland, we stayed at this school called Capability Scotland School for Crippled Children, for about four days, but it seemed like weeks. It reminded me so much of Crotched Mountain that I just sat in the library/-sitting room and cried. What went through my mind to do to Loring was shameful. I hated him for bringing me here. Why weren't we informed about this plan beforehand? Why didn't Loring give us a choice in this matter? He automatically booked it because it was cheaper for the group.

I took control of myself, I looked over my surroundings. Yes, it was just like Crotched Mountain but on a much smaller scale. The cold tiled walls, the dormitories which we had to share and divide by putting up a sheet and the complete lack of privacy all reminded me of my past. The only difference was the bathrooms which were for one person. Oh well, at least I could shit by myself! Even the cafeteria looked like an institution with long tables and bland food. We could not wait to go to town just to get a McDonald's Big Mac! And, so we did…

As the days passed by here, I could see how we were all beginning to get on each others nerves. It was like a prison in which we were all inmates. As appalling as it seems, we all had awful thoughts about Loring for placing us in this situation. I, myself, loathed him for sometime afterwards. My anger disintegrated a little only when we got on the bus to leave this dreadful place hidden by the striking, emerald grounds that surrounded it.

The one day and night in Munich was filled with beer and more beer. The night was filled with laughter and getting to know each other. At this time a volunteer, Ed, was living in Frankfort so he drove up to Munich to see me. We had met each other in the Fall of 1982 on a Boston Cerebral Palsy trip to Disney World just by sheer accident. One night after getting his charge to bed, a few of us (volunteers and charges) stayed up to chat and relax. I started to talk with him because he looked so miserable during the week. From then on, we stayed in touch for years.

However, everyone and everything changes in time. About two years ago sentimental me got in touch with Ed by computer search. It was so good to hear his voice over the telephone but it sounded weak and frail. I looked at my Personal Care Attendant at that moment with complete terror on my face. I soon found out Ed developed Multiple Scoliosis around 1994 when he was living in Germany. Thank God I did not have a picture phone because I knew I could never fake the emotion I felt after. To me Multiple Scoliosis is a death sentence. I remember this student in Hogan who had a similar disease, Muscular Dystrophy, and one day out of nowhere his place was empty without a wheelchair occupying it. The whole room was in total silence as if it was empty. In thirty seconds, I figured it out as my teacher Rob quickly wheeled me out of the classroom to talk to me while my eyes started filling up. In his gentle way he said, "Bobby passed away this morning peacefully, Gail." As I cried and screamed saying "It isn't fair!" over and over, he just sat like he did not have a classroom of students awaiting him.

Here I went again with Ed, facing my circle of fear, seeing someone else I care for wasting away and knowing what the inevitable would be. Over the course of a year or so I went up to see Ed a few times at his home in New Hampshire. The first time I saw him I was shocked at how he came walking out his front door, stumbling down the stairs. The last time I had seen him he was a big strong man but now.... I wanted to run because my heart could not handle seeing my friend in this condition. He was so frail, appearing older with sunken cheeks. But he had not lost his sense of humor and after a few minutes I was okay and happy to be there with him. I do not know if it was the Multiple Scoliosis that changed his personality, but I realized as time went on that I was always the one trying to keep the friendship together by phone or visits. He never bothered to call and when I called him it was all about him and how much pain he was in. He never seemed to care about what was going on in my life. He had good doctors that had him on pain management but he was always complaining.

During the Thanksgiving of 2006 I got the feeling that our friendship was one sided. I called him and told him how I felt. He in return told me he could care less about our friendship and was not willing to make any effort to keep it. As the months and years went on I realized he was pushing everyone away including his own family. It was like he built an invisible wall between himself and the world. I was actually shocked by this but I am glad I got to the bottom of it because I do not want nor do I need the aggravation and hurtful feelings of caring about someone I thought was a good friend that really could care less about me. Once a month or so I email his wife just to see how Ed is doing but it surely hurts. The last time I emailed, his wife, Elise, remarked "He's the captain of the boat." I wrote back "Tell him the boat is sinking fast!"

The "Captain" died on Friday, January 8, 2010...

CHAPTER 12
FREEDOM HAS ITS PRICE

It was at thirty-two years old that I found myself on a never ending merry-go-around between hiring care takers and taking my personal life into my own hands. It was during these years that I believe beyond doubt that I came to see the evils of mankind that I endured in the name of gaining my "independence." I have been robbed, raped of my self dignity, conned, scammed, lied to and abandoned by ninety percent of the people that are supposed to have been compassionate toward me, my Personal Care Attendants.

In over ninety percent of the attendants that have come and gone, I can count on one hand the ones I have trusted. I used to believe what my Personal Care Attendants told me about themselves and their loyalty towards me when they first started working for me but, as the years went on , one by one they asked for too much rope and eventually hung themselves. The ones I thought intelligent turned out to be fools and the seemingly honest faces were wearing masks to hide behind. As their masks came off I got to know that the ninety percent had more problems than I ever had in my entire life time, either due to terrible upbringings or going down the wrong paths in their lives. And, in time, of course, I took the blunt of their soiled or destructive decisions. It was I who suffered in one shape or form, whether from their work performance or terrible ethics. It was I who rode on a roller coaster as each of them walked out of my door, leaving trying to pick up the pieces of my existence. The list of the PCAs that have caused me anguish is a very long one, and would take another book to write all about it , but I truly feel it is important to share with my readers a handful of them so they can just try to put themselves in my life for awhile to think what they would do if faced with it. As the years marched on I began to believe I was a magnet to these types of personalities!

First, I soon found out that finding and searching for Personal Care Attendants was a task all by itself. If I had the money that I put into classified ads, I would be somewhat well off by now. In addition, if I had the time back that was consumed by interviews and no-show candidates, I would add years on to my life. I still do not comprehend why these individuals call, make appointments and never show up for their interviews? Through the years, I just assume they are coming but in the meantime I do my own thing. I do not sit at my dining room table twiddling my thumbs. I occupy my attention and mind playing a game of Scrabble or blackjack on my computer while the half hours fly by.

During 2001 and 2005 I had a whole deck of attendants who were strung out on drugs.

In nineteen ninety eight there was a woman who husband was killed in a truck accident prior to working for me. I had felt bad for her during the interview process so I gave her the job. After a couple of weeks I noticed that some of the pills I take periodically for my spasms were missing. My clothes started mysteriously disappearing and it just so happened that Claudia was my size. I had to let her go.

In time, I realized that a big percentage never leave my world when approximately six years later Claudia popped back into my life again by applying for a Personal Care Attendant position with my ex-girlfriend with whom I had gone to high school over thirty five years ago. The stupid ass attendant actually gave me as a reference but, on the other hand, slaughtered my whole character by telling such lies about me as being suicidal and wanting to jump over my ten storied condo balcony while she worked for me. I guess a bad penny keeps on returning!

Then there was the evening that I called "The Butter Scam" when one of my personal care attendants who was working the night shift left work to pick up butter for the lobster dinner that we were planning to have for supper that night. My intuition told me to have her leave the phone, which I can operate with my head stick, within my reach before she left . Kelli gave me some lip about it since she did not want to leave the phone where I could use it but I insisted! Hours went by and she had not returned or called. At this point I thought harm had befallen her so I called my day time personal attendant, Norma, who arrived shortly thereafter and checked my refrigerator. Lo and behold, I had butter up the yin yang. I had already waited for three hours and another hour went by before Kelli returned high as a kite. When she came in it was obvious to Norma and I that she had taken some sort of drug and had been drinking. I was furious. When I asked her where she had been she gave me this god awful story that she had been raped. I, in return, told her that she was fired. I knew it was a lie because I knew her from another job she held with a friend.

Gabrielle was recommended by her half sister, Noel, who worked for me also. Gabrielle was in turn hired. One time she brought her toddler to work, a beautiful, little girl with long, blond, unkempt hair and dressed in pajamas which were filthy. It was obvious to me that this child was not cared for properly. I found out soon enough from looking into her mother's glassy eyes that she had a serious drug problem and her daughter came second.

Ed even walked in to find out another one, Lisa, who was passed out on my living room floor from taking three sleeping pills from my bathroom medicine cabinet.

Weeks later, I heard that Lisa stolen her doctor's prescription pad from right off his desk and starting to write her own prescriptions.

My path has also been crossed by several con artists. ,women who have been professional in the interview process but then have shown their true colors a couple of weeks to a couple of months into the job. It is all a matter of how smart they thought they were. Con artists clothed in the personal care attendant façade use a common practice, which is to tell me over and over again, day in and day out, how much they love me. It sounds so insincere to begin with that I have always had the feeling that there will be trouble to follow. I have heard it all.

I hired Nanci in the spring of 2006. Her mannerisms and presentation during her inter-view were impeccable. Two weeks into the job I received a phone call from her. She said she sprained her ankle falling into a dinner plate sized pothole while at the supermarket. Joy had to work her shift that week while she was at the doctors. I came to find out she had gone to Connecticut for that weekend afterwards and told her boyfriend to call for her. Needless to say she let me down due to her irresponsible behavior which was underneath the mature, reliable woman she claimed to be. She left me high and dry and it took me weeks to find a replacement. If I could have had one wish I would wish I could read these idiots' minds in the beginning and foresee the bullshit they hide within themselves, only to try and use it on me later. I just felt I was being taken advantage of and they thought they could actually get away with their actions without any penalty at all.

I had hired a woman I give the name Lynne in the autumn of 2002. I had no clue of what was to come. This experience was the turning point of my life. I ended up being psychologically abused and mentally harassed by her when a sexual incident happened and subsequent demands for hours were placed upon me. This haunted me for years and I never told a soul, not even my mother. I ask myself to this day why had not I seen it coming and then I realize it takes a lifetime of learning through experience before anyone wakes up to the harsh realities of life.

And on and on it goes…

In between 1986-1990 an acquaintance of my sister became a Personal Care Attendant. Jackie was ten years younger than me and we had more in common. Jackie wanted to go out nights and relax also. I had an ally with Jackie at the nightclubs and I felt pretty good at the time because we had a lot of fun together. We were also roommates as I needed care full time round the clock, but things were not as they seemed with her. As time went by she started acting odd. I could never find my bills or mail and come to find out she had stuffed them into my kitchen drawer unopened. I didn't realize this until I got FINAL NOTICE on some of my bills. I was livid!

In time I requested a two bedroom apartment, because, as it was, I was sleeping on a very uncomfortable sofa bed for years. We moved to a bigger apartment in the same building sometime after so we could each have a bedroom. The two bedroom apartment was mine because I paid all the bills and I was the renter. Somehow, Jackie did not see it this way because on the same day that we got there she asked me if she could have the bigger bedroom with the air conditioner. It was a very forward request for someone who was not paying the bills. I used to go to stay at my parents three nights a week so she could do her own thing on her days off. I tested her to see if she slept in my bed while I was gone by placing a quarter between the bottom and top sheets. If it moved, I knew she slept in my bed. Sure enough she had! Another issue was the air conditioner. Secretly, I had my brother take off a wire on the air conditioner. Sure enough she had used my bed and also had called maintenance to fix the air conditioner.

Another incident happened when she invited a friend of hers that lived in Pennsylvania to stay for a weekend. Her friend also had a three year old child. She had not bothered to ask me how I felt about her plans so when I confronted her she started to pull a tantrum on me. I soon learned she could not deal with confrontation like many people. She either started the tears flowing or ran. Once on a trip to Scotland with the Boston Cerebral Palsy Group, she made a dig to me about not buying her a leather jacket. I guess it did not cross her mind on how she got there! She sure did not hitch hike! I paid for her entire trip. She made a joke out of this situation as she always did with every confrontation we had. "I was only kidding," she laughed.

There was one particular action she did I cannot ever forget. We were in Rome and I happened to have a sick stomach. I guess it didn't matter to her because she went out sightseeing while I lay in a strange bed, hoping and praying I wouldn't shit the bed.

Yes, Jackie was a piece of work, but to this day I still can not comprehend why she ever did these things to me because otherwise we were like sisters. Still to this day, twelve years later, she does not admit any wrong doings on her part at all.

Dear Jackie,

    I have been putting off the writing of this letter for a year or so now, but, I think it's due. And, I am ready. Many things have been bothering me, and I just feel that just talking face-to face with one another wouldn't do. I know it wouldn't accomplish anything. I hope by writing my thoughts on paper will clear my mind a little. I think it is the best way to go, because, the written word has a power of its own which can't be interrupted or denied. I think I'll start from the most recent events. I shall begin last March after your trouble with Steve. It was here that I started hearing rumors about me. Rumors like: "Job was "unreliable," Pay was "unreliable." According to my memory you were the one who quit on her own. I never did "fire" you. You were told that the job could be left on hold until you put your life together no matter how many weeks it took. It was you who made the decision to leave. I had no part in the move that you made. You had all of these new and grand plans like going to school, etc., etc. When everything fell through your excuses were there weren't any child day care, etc., etc., etc This was a lie, because people on Medicaid get automatic child care.

Secondly, the accusation over the "pay being "unreliable" is an incorrect one. Except for one single week prior to your departure, Jackie, when I believe I stayed in Danvers, be-cause of a cold, there were not any weeks that you were "unpaid". Looking back through the years the job/pay were so "unreliable" that you received ALL of your pay WHENEVER you WERE sick: cold, sore throat, etc., OR laid-up with you're ankle, foot, back and the list goes on. You were paid even if you stayed an extra fifteen minutes. That was pretty good for a job that was so "un-reliable." I can even say half pay was given to you all of the "Summer of '88" which was free and clear, where no bills, rent, etc. had to be thought about. The funniest thing to this story is when you asked me two years later for "retroactive" pay for the Summer of 1988 I realized weeks later what your motive was, Jackie. Sometimes it took me time to have something sink in!!!

Anyways, the answer amounted to you were 2 1/2 mos. pregnant at the time: June 22, '90, and, of course, you needed money for this blessed happening, etc., etc. It was just fine that you were looking out for yourself, Jackie, but, when you made up an entirely different story when confronted later put the icing on the cake. Your answer when confronted was: "I meant for the Ship week." This trip which took place Dec. '88 - Jan. '89. A week vs. 8 weeks? ? ?? Did or do you really think I'm that stupid? Did you think I was that ignorant not to had figured this scheme out? I would had thought more of you if you just came out with the fact that you were pregnant and was worried financial wise, Jackie. Just the truth would had done more than some little lies.

Finally there remains little incidents throughout the years that still stick in my mind. These things should never had happened amongst so-called friends living and working together for five years under the same roof.

The first was the giving of my bedroom to you in the old apt. while I slept out on the sofa couch. As I said, this was my doing. But, when you expected to have the "big" bedroom in the new apt., even asking if we could draw straws, I just couldn't get over the nerve. I, the prime occupant, the person who paid the rent, etc., etc., had to be confronted like this to who would get the master bed-room? From the right standpoint, there should never have been any question or inquiry on this issue at all. I knew a lot of talk went on over this when your mother

commented on who got the bedroom on moving
day. Lastly, there were just little minor
things that you did which got to me, Jackie.
One of the MANY incidents was the indications
you were sleeping in my bed, because, of
your very concerning attitude about the air
conditioner not working. I can't forget how
strongly you wanted to call the office. I
just passed it off saying I never used it,
etc.,etc., which was the truth.

Another happening was when you invited
your girlfriend, Elaine, & daughter to stay
at my apt. WITHOUT even giving it a second
thought of asking me... You just took it on
your own to invited these people, who I didn't
even know, to stay the weekend at MY home,
to sleep in MY beds, to eat from MY kitchen.
WITHOUT EVEN ASKING ME. I can just recall
my reaction after the phone call, you going
to the kitchen, coming up with the solution
of your dilemma being, they would stay in
Steve's apt., and then all hell broke out.
It was fine and dandy for strangers to be
in my apt., but, when Steve's territory was
being invaded, he came to his own defense. It
was funny, Jackie, how when it involved his
property and domain, it was wrong, but, a few
minutes prior Steve cared less on where your
friend laid her hat. God only knows where
they stayed that weekend ? ? ?

My question is "Why, Jackie???" Why all of
the games, the lies, the deception throughout
the years??? It was so good living and
working with you 95% of the time. We had SO
many good times. You are like a sister to
me. You took so great care of me. I say you
are close if you have a per-son wiping your

ass everyday!!!! We were ALWAYS there for one another during ALL of the turmoil in our lives. AND, WE BOTH HAD SOME TURMOILS DURING THOSE SIX YEARS! This is the reason I just CAN'T comprehend why you did these things. Some minor, but, they were still games. Games which you DIDN'T need to play, at all, Jackie. Not amongst two people, NEVERTHELESS, two very, close friends. Just TRY to make me understand??? That's all.

Maybe the bottom line was you made moves without thinking? ? ?

I am making the first move in my conscience, a conscience that has been bothering me for years. No one should have or hold any conflict or dislike for another person. I'm afraid I have been guilty of this for years. How are we going to start to resolve these conflicts is up to you now,

Jackie.

I only know I have a load lifted off my shoulders, a load which has haunted me for years now. I hope our friendship can be put back together again.

See you soon.

Love,

Gail

Between 1990 and 1993, I had to hire other attendants to take over some of Jackie's hours because she became pregnant and had to get married. One of them was Norma. I remember the day she came for the interview. She pranced in all dressed to the nines with a briefcase on her arm. My sister and I thought she was in the wrong apartment. I believe she thought the same when she saw that we had drinks in front of us and offered her one! She looked baffled that a woman with a disability in a wheelchair would be having a cocktail. I do not remember why, but she was hired on the spot. I needed her full time until Jackie was back from her pregnancy leave. Being disabled I have always been very conscious about my health. Norma was a chain smoker and never went outside to smoke. My life became like a circus, surrounded by clowns, with a strange man crawling around my balcony at all hours of the night, because the man Norma was seeing did not have the sense to come through the front door. I nearly got kicked out of my apartment because of them. She worked for me for five years ,during which time I met Ed. I noticed a change in her behavior when Ed came into my life. I guess she thought I had no life save her because she appeared jealous when Ed was around.

One night when she was on call, I asked her to come over at eight o'clock to help me get dressed because the three of us were going to the Porthole Restaurant to eat. In the meantime, a short time before eight, Ed helped me onto the bathroom. I figured I would save us some time when she came. She came alright… a quarter past nine o'clock she walked through the door as I was stark naked and fit to be tied because she had purposely tried to ruin the evening. I held back my temper and stayed cool. She asked me why I was not dressed and I responded by telling her that she was supposed to have been there at eight to dress me. She was playing a head game with me because we talked on her cell phone two and a half hours prior while she was driving home from her daughter's. I took notice of the time because I was getting ready to watch 60 Minutes. As Norma entered my apartment two hours and fifteen minutes later, I knew she had other plans earlier that evening because she was dressed up like she was going to a wedding or to have a rendezvous with her friend, Zorba, the same man I found crawling around my balcony years prior. About nine years passed until, again, Norma came back to work for me. It did not work out the second time around either as will be explained later on in my story. Norma and I to this day are still friends, but it is like oil and water working together. We have had our ups and downs over the years and probably always will. We are total opposites.

I had a full deck of attendants during the years of 1990 through 1996. In all my years of playing cards with my sister I had only seen two jokers per deck, yet in my deck there were many, too many! It sometimes seemed like a revolving door to me, which I never quite got used to. Although I have tried to understand people for a long, long time, I must admit to myself that I never really will. Unfortunately, the use of personal care attendants was needed for me in order to maintain my independence. I suddenly realized that my independence came with an extremely high price tag and I am not talking money here. Oh no, it came with many strings attached and I had more than a few cankers on my tongue from biting it so hard, so often.

An example of this came in the form of a mother and daughter team. Betsy, the mother, worked days and Cher did the three to eleven shifts. The two of them worked out very well. The both of them took great care of me I have to admit. But as time went on, I realized Cher had some inner problems which affected my life. One night she left the job, leaving me alone from eleven p.m. until nine o'clock in the morning while she went home to her boyfriend and daughter. I felt like a character in the movie "Home Alone," only this time I was not being confronted by burglars, but a fear of being absolutely helpless in my own apartment.

There were times when my attendants would just leave me high and dry by quitting on the spot. I even had to go with Ed to his work more than a few times because of thoughtless people that never showed up when scheduled.

At one point in my life I was living in an apartment complex that was home to not only people with disabilities but the elderly as well. My unit was on the sixth floor. Lita, a Greek woman who was in her late fifties, was hired as my PCA. She was an exceptionally kind woman but we differed in personality and knowledge. Sometimes I felt like her mentor telling her that certain television programs were simply acts like the Jerry Springer Show which was all staged in advance , but she never believed me. During those times, I retreated into the den to go on my computer where I could get a piece of my sanity back. Other times, Lita could make me laugh until I thought I would pee myself. Those times were always in the bathroom when she showered me. There weren't any accessible bathrooms in the complex and so she had to lift me over the tub to place me in my shower chair. She was completely able to lift me, but not when we got laughing.

My body went completely limp and I was unable to help her at all. Yes, we had some good laughs together.

There was only one incident which I was really surprised at. I had recently bought a Bichon Frise puppy named Champion which needed to be taken down in the elevator and walked outside. Lita decided to let my puppy roam the hallways one afternoon as she checked on my laundry. Being a puppy he had a field day jumping up on the old folks that were coming and going from the lobby. The next day I received a phone call from the office telling me I was being evicted. I had no idea what they were talking about. "What the hell had I done?" When I was told that my puppy was loose in the lobby jumping on people with walkers I knew Lita had to be responsible for this. I called her right away with a not too pleasant tone in my voice and told her what the office had told me. She started to cry and proceeded to call my mother, telling my mother I was "yell-ing" at her. In turn my mother called me and asked me what the hell was going on as if I had done something wrong! Lita showed up for work the next day and I calmly had to explain to her the consequences of her actions and the trouble she had caused me. The woman did not know any better, but I was able to keep my apartment thank God.

Then came Dianne who was a hot ticket, but a bit rough around the edges. She turned out to be lazy as hell. She sat around my condo day to day watching her soap operas. Funny thing is at the same time she wanted more money.

Terry worked for me during the summer of 1999. She only worked for me a couple of afternoons a week between three and six. She had another job working full time in a nursing home at the same time she worked for me. She was soon acting like my mother or guardian because she gave me grief when I asked for my afternoon cocktail. In fact, she went so far as to tell other home health workers in the city in which I lived that I was a drunk! She had left her job with me with the "sad" excuse that she had to leave to take care of her sister who supposedly had fallen down some stairs. Although I knew she was lying due to the fact of how in the hell was she going to survive without working, I was glad to be rid of her.

A young woman from Jamaica then came and took care of cooking my suppers in the afternoons. Michelle was a doll. Unlike the others, she had class. Not only was she respectful and polite to me, she also looked out for my best interests, not just what she could get from me.

I had a woman working for me that was bringing her newborn baby to work. As can be imagined Koko took care of the needs of her baby instead of mine. She even went so far as to bring her dirty laundry to work without asking me. I had no clothes to wear because the baby's diapers were in my washing machine while my clothes sat in the hamper. I had to let her go.

I have had aides expect me to pay for lunch when we went out. This one aide, in particular, Maria, had her boyfriend come along for the dinner I was giving to her as a birthday gift. Ed was with us and at the end of our meal Ed took the check and added it up to include Maria's meal, assuming her boyfriend was going to pay for his own. Not only had her boyfriend caused a scene at the table when he ordered a dish he didn't like but he never offered to chip in for his share of the check. A funny thing happened an hour later when we went out for drinks and the money to play Keno came flowing out of his pocket. I was taken advantage of a lot by my aides and their friends.

Another time one of my aides had her daughter join us for lunch one day. When the check came, Nancy took MY cash out of MY wallet to pay for everything!

Nancy had a friend who also worked as a fill in. She did not work with me for long. It was an experience in the long run. I refer to her as "The Wallpaper Queen." Dottie offered to hang wallpaper in my bathroom. As money was never discussed I took it to mean she was doing it as part of her wages. It turned out horrible, as seams were coming away from the wall and at some spots overlapping each other. She did all this during her regular work hours and I had not asked her to do it. Yet within the next few weeks she expected to be paid above and beyond her paycheck.

I had a young woman working for me who mentally and psychologically abused her children right in front of my eyes. Noel had brought her eleven year old daughter and her year and a half old son to work with her one day. The older child asked for help with her homework and her baby son was crying. She took her hand and smacked both of them really hard on the head. Today I would be approaching it with a telephone call to Department of Social Services.

I regretted the time I hired two male attendants. One of them came from Haiti . He disappeared with my dog, Champion, for two hours to God knows where while the second one made advances toward me. I have not hired a man since!

Then there are those aides that have treated me like a child. As a college graduate it angers me to no end that just because I am physically disabled, some treat me as being mentally disabled as well. Cerebral Palsy affects people in different ways. While there are many of those which are afflicted mentally, there are different areas of the brain that control our bodies as well. Most people do not realize this.

One aide that comes to mind was a middle age woman named Dawn. She treated me like a patient with dementia. Statements such as "Smile!" and "Be happy!" kept coming out of her mouth. If I had use of my arms I would have thrown something at her. Here I was concentrating on the business of the day and she thought it her place to interrupt my thoughts with a stupid, irritating suggestion that I ought to be smiling all day. What a pain in the ass she became. She only lasted an afternoon and a half, approximately five hours. That was as much as I could take from her.

With the popularity of cell phones, I have had instances where my aides have been so busy with their cell phone calls or texting that their work was ignored. Doris, Christine and Anna were good examples of that. I especially got a kick out of Doris, who text -messaged throughout the six or so weeks that she was working here while at the same time she sat at my dining room table with me while leafing through the pile of catalogs she lugged along with her every day. As the hours dragged by, I felt like I was paying them for nothing! Around half past four every afternoon all of their cell phones would start ringing like chimes of The Sistine Chapel and I lost attention completely. I was tolerant of this for years, until Anna came in the summer of 2007. Her phone sounded like an ice cream truck from years back when I was a kid. I always did wonder how she felt when I posted rules on the refrigerator in the morning?!

For ALL P.C.A.'s :

1. **ALL CELL PHONES TO BE PLACED IN MY BACKPACK UPON ENTRANCE!**

   No incoming or outgoing telephone calls (EXCEPT FOR EMERCENCIES) during one's shift.

2. **All cell phones to be turned off as soon employees begin shift. Cell messages may be checked a couple of times per day. (NO GIVING OUT MY TELEPHONE**

   NUMBER FOR PERSONAL REA

3. **Each PCA has "3" breaks during a 8 hour shift.**

   Each PCA has "1" break during a 4 hour shift.

4. **Please be sure I know where you are as I may need you for something, except when outside.**

So far as of today: Tuesday, October 10, 2007, Anna had broken three of them...

I found out as the months went traveling by that Anna was her own worst enemy, but she wanted everyone else to suffer for her life's mistakes. Due to my own stupidity I eventually became one of her victims. She was a single mother with two daughters in their teens that were a handful so once again I became ensnared in her unstructured world. Between coming to work late half of the time and complaining to me about not getting paid for hours she never was here actually working, I had just had it with her. I foolishly opened a Wal-Mart credit card for her so she could get Christmas gifts for her little brats. I guess I learned a lesson as the weeks went on when each time I called the credit card company the amount was also going up. She proclaimed I would get paid for all of it but I had not even gotten paid for her purchase of my two year old computer , which came with numerous software programs which would had cost her double if she purchased it brand new in a store.

As of Tuesday, December 11, 2007, she claimed she had fallen in the driveway hitting her tail bone but she was able to go down and up cellar stairs retrieving her kids' Christmas presents and I am struck with the six hundred and seventy dollar bill.

In the evening of Wednesday, December 12th , two days allegedly after falling in my driveway, Anna called saying , "I'll come to work Friday." I fired her at this time knowing she was a habitual liar and con artist if I ever saw one in my life. Weeks later I found out I was right again as she conned me out of eighty-six dollars from my own pocket.

She concocted up this believable story that she called Boston Center for Independent Living and talked to the head of the PCA's Program, telling her that I was obligated to pay for her hours at the Emergency Room visit the day that she fell. There is not any proof of this fall, because she never filed for workers' compensation and she has been working right along in a new job. A new job where there are new opportunities for Mrs. Anna to steal and suck people dry.

CHAPTER 13

A NEW BEGINNING

Gail Sanfilippo

It was Sunday, August 05, 2007 and as I listened to the constant flow of cars go pass my residence, I wondered where each of them was going and what they have to face in life. I guess we all have a story to tell and this is mine.

My life turned out very different than I had expected two years ago. I thought Joy would be a friend and a comrade for years and years to come, but this will never be. Despite how good she was to me, she took advantage of my weakness by controlling her role over me. She crossed the line, so to say, between employer and employee, as so many of my attendants did. It mainly began when I found out that 3/4 of my pain medication was gone from when I had broken my leg on my vacation in Aruba in September of 2006 while being lifted into a cab. Months later she automatically assumed she could sniff lines of cocaine at my dining room table.

My story continued with Joy as the months rolled by and I watched Joy's downward spiral in her personal and professional life. She herself admitted she had problems, saying she needed to find herself. She truly was finding herself, or I should say, destroying her life.

Joy really went downhill in the summer of 2007. She frequently called in sick with symptoms like headaches, stiff neck and high fevers which varied in degrees each time I talked to her over the phone. First her temperature was 99.9 degrees, than as the story continued, she claimed herself dead, little did she realize, with a temp up to over 108.0 degrees.

So off she went to the doctor's, finding out she might have had Homophiles Influenza Type B (HIB) which is a form of meningitis. Hallmarks of meningitis are fever, decreased mental stability, stiff neck and swelling of the throat. As I researched HIB on my computer and read on, I fearfully acknowledged Joy was complaining of sore throats and neck stiffness during that period of time, too. As far as her mental instability, it was always at question for me over the past two years with her ups and downs, highs and lows each day that she worked here. She could be as happy and funny as she was low and depressed. Truthfully, every time she came through the door, I honestly never knew how she was going to be. All I knew was that her moods were controlled by drugs whether they were legal or not. It is quite a scary thought looking back on it.

As I studied about HIB, I came to a complete standstill when I read that the disease could possibly be transmitted to others by the spread of respiratory droplets. It was here that I really lost Joy or she lost me, when I said to her by a simple phone call that she could have the next day off prior to my vacation. I did not want to expose myself at that time or at anytime in the near future to the illness, especially when she needed to be in close proximity to me when showering, dressing and feeding me. I even emailed my doctor.

-----Original Message-----
From: Gail4000@aol.com [mailto:Gail4000@aol.com]
Sent: Monday, July 23, 2007 12:52 PM
To: Braun, Edward M.,M.D.Subject: Question Regarding HIB

Dr. Braun,

One of my PCA's mentioned that she may have been infected with HIB. However, she did not tell me directly. She has been going to the doctor for some time and has been sick a lot lately. Her doctor told her that she should get vaccines for HIB. Because of this, I am now worried that I might be a risk, as well as my other PCA's. The symptoms of the PCA are fever, a stiff neck, and a very bad sore throat.

I do not know if you have all my medical records, but if you do, I was wondering if I ever received an HIB vaccine or the vaccine for bacterial meningitis. If I have had them, would I be at risk of anything? If I haven't had them, what should I do now to avoid any risks?

I am going away Wednesday morning, so I would really appreciate it if you got back to me as soon as possible. I really hope to hear from you soon, because I am very worried.

Thank you,

Gail Sanfilippo

Dear Ms. Sanfilippo,

HIB? What do we mean by that? Also, is the PCA in hospital? Does she actually have meningitis? If so, this is a reportable illness to the State Health Department and you should be contacted and get information through the PCA's employer, as well as antibiotic prophylaxis if this was warranted.

You have never had the vaccine.

Dr Braun

I am slowly coming to the knowledge that people in general are their own worst enemies. Joy is one of them. One August 8th she got arrested and was committed to Salem Hospital's suicide unit. I know this because she called me from there. As I listened to her, I knew she was lying to herself and to the world as she repeatedly said to me "I was only swimming, Gail. It is the anniversary of my brother, Jay's, death." As she chattered on, I could hear her being literally tied down by hospital staff while her voice became faint in the distance. It was the most disturbing call I received since a week before my Cousin Terry's suicide eight years ago when she had reached out to me for help. Over the next two days there was no news from Joy at all, so I figured no news was good news, but I was wrong. When the phone rang Friday indicating "Private number" I knew it was her. How I dreaded hearing her familiar voice which sounded like nothing had happened during the past two days. I soon got to know the "real" Joy on August 10, 2007 when I called after supper not knowing it would be my last telephone call to her. We talked but this time she was in complete denial about everything except the taking of my leg pain medication. And, I mean, everything from her actions on the job to her personal life with her live-in boyfriend who is a coke dealer at a bar in their town.

Regretfully, I lost my temper, telling her that it was all over. She slammed the receiver before I could say anything like I was one of her doormats. She just hung up the phone as though I was a telemarketer trying to sell something to her.

As anyone would guess, this was not the end of this ridiculous fiasco. Between getting mail with no return address, different handwriting on envelopes and numerous telephone calls from a "Private Number," echoing through my mind, I had to think of myself for once and called the Lynnfield Police to file a criminal complaint against her because I was fearful of what she would do next.

Although, the calls stopped on August 30th, when I had all "Private Calls" blocked, I STILL look over my shoulder at the phone when it starts ringing and wonder what may be her next move. . .

The saddest thing is I would never have thought Joy would be out of my life so soon. The song by Carole King "Now and Forever" sums up my relationship with Joy. She will always be a part of me. I miss the laughter and the tears. If anyone had told me one and half years ago that Joy would be out of my life so soon, I would have laughed in their faces, thinking they were nuts. I thought I knew better, but I knew nothing. They foresaw better what I never saw but who knows what is actually going on in a person's mind?

At the time, I just had to open up my mind to the awful reality that she was like 90% of all my personal care workers. Sadly, I can compare all my attendants to characters in B rated movies where you watch and wonder if, as director, we could change them to have better endings ...

Then I start thinking about my life, which was not a piece of cake or an easy paved road to travel down. How come I made it without leaving pathways of destruction or forsaken my soul for others to pickup? What makes me different then most individuals who have strolled through my front door for the past twenty-three years? I truly think I owe 90% of it to how I was brought up with so much love and discipline. The remaining 10% I attribute to my own strength of character and determination not to fail. This is the difference. Most are individuals who have traveled down wrong roads and have not been able to get out of their own self-destruction, feeding on others for their survival and worth.

All I know is that because of them I cannot trust anybody and even doubt my own judgment. After approximately twenty-three years of living independently, I've become privy to the knowledge of the many strings attached. Whatever my attendants go through in their personal lives, from terrible and unhealthy childhoods to bad marriages, it always comes into the workplace with them, unfortunately resulting in my physical and psychological suffering.

Everyone had his/her own struggles and demons in life but the key is the way each one deals with what's upon one's plate. One can take different roads in a lifetime but it's the road you choose which determines how you will be remembered. Every path I have chosen has been a climb. It will always be a climb, but it's always going to be another mountain and I'm always going to want to make the climb. I believe the "climb" has made me into the better person I am today, whether there were battles with others or the struggles I found within myself. Each one has carved its memory into my heart, and I hope has made its impression upon you as well. Always strive for the best you can be and life and it will return the favor in kind.

THE END

CPSIA information can be obtained at www.ICGtesting.com
230889LV00005B/117/P